MY DAY! MY DREAM! MY DESTINY!

Date:

To:

From:

Message:

You Can Do More Than Survive, You Can Succeed!

EVERY DAY AN EASY A

Food Is for the Body
Education Is for the Mind
Poetry Is for the Soul

Sharon Esther Lampert

The Restless Sunrise

A Streaming Golden Light
Enters In and Under the Windowsill

A Restless Sleeper
Is Awakened to New Beginnings

To Catch a Sunrise
The Dreamer Arises as the Light Bursts Forth

The Sunrise Lights Up the Sky
In Anticipation of a World

That Has Yet To Be Created.

Sharon Esther Lampert

Also By The Author

Student Empowerment Tools
for Academic Success

- EVERY DAY AN EASY A
- TOTAL RECALL: ACE EVERY TEST EVERY TIME
- Your Study Room Is Under New Management
- Smartgrades School Notebooks with 1000 Learning Tools
- WRITERS RUN THE WORLD: College English Bootcamp!
- LEARN ENGLISH

Parent Empowerment Tools
for Academic Success

- How to Parent for Academic Success
- Broken Wings Blocked Blessings

Teacher Empowerment Tools
for Academic Success

- The Silent Crisis Destroying America's Brightest Minds
  ("Book of the Month" Alma Public Library, Wisconsin)

- The Universal Gold Standard of Education

- How Does Learning Take Place

Psychological Empowerment Tools
for Academic Success

- Integration Therapy: 14 Steps to True and Everlasting Happiness
- How to Stop Paying for the Sins of Your Parents
- Lost, Bad, and Evil: The Root of All Evil Is Child Abuse

Children's Book
The Smartest Children's Book In The Whole World
Learn New Vocabulary with **Color-Coded** Words

SCHMALTZY: IN AMERICA EVEN A CAT CAN HAVE A DREAM

The Cat Who Helps Children Learn, Love, and Laugh
THE WORLD FAMOUS PIANO VIRTUOSO
BOOKWORM CHILDREN'S BOOK AWARD
schmaltzy.com

EVERY DAY AN EASY A

SHARON ROSE SUGAR

SMARTGRADES
BRAIN POWER REVOLUTION
www.smartgrades.com

EVERY DAY AN EASY A

College Edition
- Hardcover ISBN: 978-1-885872-97-5
- Paperback ISBN: 978-1-885872-98-2
- E-Book ISBN: 978-1-885872-14.2

Library of Congress Catalog Card Number: 2007902045
UPC: 672180

SMARTGRADES
BRAIN POWER REVOLUTION

Smartgrades.com
EverydayanEasyA.com
PhotonSuperhero.com
BooksnotBombs.com
Schmaltzy.com
SharonEstherLampert.com
WorldFamousPoems.com

SMARTGRADES books may be purchased for education,
business, or sales promotional use.

To Order Books:
Ingram, Phone: 615-793-5000
Baker and Taylor, Phone: 800-775-1800

Book Interior and Cover Design By Sharon Esther Lampert
Illustrations: By Mark A. Hicks, illustrator. Used with permission.
For more information, please visit websites:
www.MARKIX.net and www.markix.net/4teachers.html

First Edition

Manufactured in the United States of America

8 Goalposts of Education

1. Education: Knowledge!
2. Enlightenment: AHA!
3. Empowerment: Yes I Can!
4. Excellence: Mastery!
5. Emancipation: All Can Do!
6. Egalitarianism: Equal Rights!
7. Equality: New World Order!
8. Economic Stability: World Peace!

Sharon Rose Sugar

The Paladin of Education for the 21st Century

To earn your diploma, every teacher will ask you to perform the same four academic tasks over and over again, day in and day out, week in and week out, and year in and year out.

1. Read a Chapter
2. Write a Paper
3. Solve a Problem
4. Take a Test

Sharon Rose Sugar

The Paladin of Education for the 21st Century

THIS BOOK SAVES LIVES

"The Silent Crisis Destroying America's Brightest Minds"
"Book of the Month" Alma Public Library, Wisconsin

READ, WRITE, SOLVE, TEST

EVERY DAY AN EASY A

SMARTGRADES

SUCCESS STRATEGY STUDY SKILLS

Our books include the **SMARTGRADES** Learning Skills and Life **Skills** that will empower you for academic success in school, personal succcess at home, and professional success in the workplace.

SMARTGRADES Time Management Skills:
- Homework Action Planner
- To Do List Tool
- Setting Priorities Tool
- Divide and Conquer Tool
- Estimate and Actual Time Log Tool
- Speedbumps: Detours, Delays, and Distractions Tool

SMARTGRADES In-Class Skills:
- Prereading Tool
- Active Listening Tool
- Note Taking Tool
- Abbreviation Tool
- Questioning Tool
- Test Preview Question Tool

SMARTGRADES At-Home Skills:
- Organization Tool
- School Notebooks with **SMARTGRADES SUCCESS STRATEGY**
- Study Room Tool
- Study Strategy Tool
- Subject Strategy Tool
- Power Study Snack Tool
- Manage Anxiety, Stress, and Depression

SMARTGRADES Reading Skills:
- Speed Reading Tool
- Reading Comprehension Tool

SMARTGRADES Test Preparation Skills:
- 10 Step Processing Tools for Instant & Total Recall

SMARTGRADES Writing Skills:

- Outlining Tool
- Annotating Tool
- Summarizing Tool
- Paraphrasing Tool
- English Essay Tool
- Research Paper Tool
- Citation Tool
- Proofreading to Perfection Tool

SMARTGRADES Thinking Skills:

- Critical Thinking Tool
- Creative Thinking Tool **WORLD PREMIERE!**
- Scientific Thinking Tool
- Mathematical Thinking Tool

SMARTGRADES On-Test Skills:

- Multiple Choice Tool
- Essay Exam Tool
- True False Tool
- Matching Tool
- Fill In the Blank Tool
- Identity Exam Tool
- Verbal Analogy Tool
- Oral Exam Tool
- Open Book Tool
- Take Home Tool
- Standardized Exam Tool

SMARTGRADES Career Skills: (College Edition)

- Career and Personality Tool
- Summer Internship & Life Experience Tool
- Networking Tool
- Entrepreneur Tool
- Job Tool
- Career Tool

Sugar's 7 Grade A Facts of Academic Success

Fact 1. Your Brain Is a Powerful Biological Machine
Put your hands on your head and feel your brain. Your brain is the most powerful biological machine in the world. This book is your instruction manual and will show you how to maximize your brain power. Facts are food for the brain. You will spend most of your day eating facts and building your brain muscles. First, you will retrieve facts from your teacher. Second, you will process the facts using the new learning technology, **SMART-GRADES SUCCESS STRATEGY.** Third, you will return the facts to the teacher in a essay, research paper, or on a test.

Fact 2. Eat Right for the Energy to Learn (Chapter 3)
Before you can feed your brain the facts, you have to feed your body for the energy to learn. Healthy meals consist of carbohydrates, protein, fresh fruits and vegetables containing vitamins and minerals. To maximize your energy to learn, you will need sufficient sleep, good eating habits, and regular exercise. Junk food won't cut it. Avoid eating foods loaded with addictive sugar and salt and processed with chemicals that are devoid of natural vitamins and minerals.

Fact 3. The First Week of School (Chapter 1)
It only takes the first week of school for students to fall behind and start playing catch-up. You have to learn how to manage your time, and make every hour count.

Fact 4. School Is All About the Facts, Not About You
Your job is to **RETRIEVE** the facts from the class notes, handouts, and textbook, and then **RETURN** the facts to the teacher in an essay, research paper, and on a test.

Fact 5. The 80/20 Rule (Chapter 7)

If you can send back 80% of the facts for a B grade, then you can send back the remaining 20% of the facts for an A grade. If you process the facts for long-term retention using the new learning technology, **SMARTGRADES SUCCESS STRATEGY,** then you will have Instant & Total Recall of all of the facts.

Fact 6. What Are the Critical Hours of the School Day?

- Class Time: 1 Hour (fixed)
- Study Period: 2-6 Hours (variable)
- Test Time: 1 Hour (fixed)

Fact 7. Every Day of the Week Is Test Preparation Day

Priority #1 Did you sleep well, eat right, and exercise for the energy to learn? (Chapter 3)

Priority #2 Do you have a SMARTGRADES **Homework Action Planner** to organize your life? (Chapter 1 & 2)

Priority #3 Do you have SMARTGRADES **School Notebooks 2N1, 3N1,** and **4N1** with learning tools to achieve academic success? (Chapter 4)

Priority #4 Right after class, did you write Test-Review Notes and process the facts using your **SMARTGRADES SUCCESS STRATEGY** for Instant & Total Recall to ace a test? (Chapter 7)

10 Step SMARTGRADES Success Strategy Tools to Ace Tests

Step 1. Estimation	Step 6. Association
Step 2. Divide and Conquer	Step 7. Test-Review Notes
Step 3. Active Reading	Step 8. Conversion
Step 4. Extraction	Step 9. Visualization
Step 5. Condensation	Step 10. Self-Test

SUPERHIGHWAY OF ACADEMIC SUCCESS

1. School Is All About the Facts

2. The Facts Are Always on the Move

In Class
Facts Move from a Blackboard into a Notebook

At Home
Facts Move into a Test Review Note,
Homework Assignment, Essay, and Research Paper

On Test
Facts Move Through Your Brain for Instant
and Total Recall and onto a Test

Education Is Measured by 3 Criteria:

In-Depth Comprehension

Long Term Retention

Mastery of the Material

Sharon Rose Sugar

The Paladin of Education for the 21st Century

THIS BOOK SAVES LIVES

"The Silent Crisis Destroying America's Brightest Minds"
"Book of the Month" Alma Public Library, Wisconsin

EVERYBODY IS SOMEBODY SPECIAL

Keep in Touch!
Photon@PhotonSuperhero.com

Name: PHOTON

Born: Planet Lumina
Planet Lumina Is in the Halo
Galaxy Where all Angels Are Born

My Two Super Powers:
Left Eye Is a Human Telescope
Right Eye Is a Human Microscope

My Mission:
To place new learning technology
10 STEP SMARTGRADES
SUCCESS STRATEGY
STUDY SKILLS
Directly into the Hands of All
Earthling Students to Empower
Them for Academic Success!

My Spaceship:
The Intergalactic Radiant

WORLD PEACE IS COMING TO PLANET EART

Your Instruction Manual

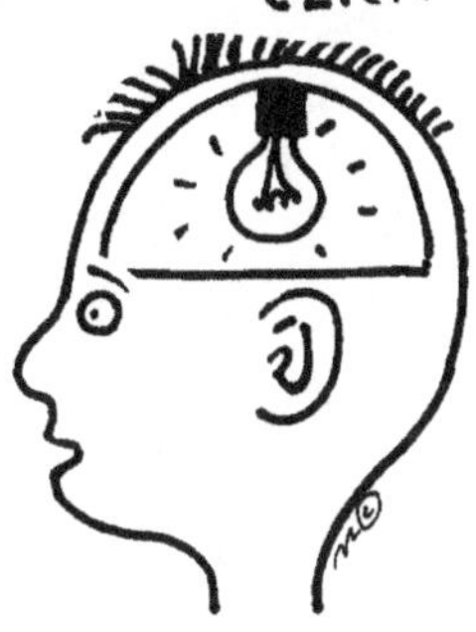

Put Your Hands on Your Head.
Your Brain Is the Most Powerful
Biological Machine in the World.
Your Brain Is Your Most Valuable Asset.
This Book Is the Instruction Manual for Your Brain.

Facts Are Food for Your Brain.
School Is a Restaurant and Facts Are on the Menu.
Eat the Facts and Build Your Brain Muscle.
Knowledge Is Power, Purpose, Passion, and Prosperity.
Good Grades Deserve Great Rewards.
In 24 Hours, Earn A Grade and Free Gift!

Make the Grade and Achieve Your Dream!
Every Student Is a Success Story!
Every Student Is Somebody Special!
MY DAY! MY DREAM! MY DESTINY!
LIVE YOUR DREAMS!

If You Need My Help, I Am at Your Service,

www.PhotonSuperhero.com

MY DAY!
MY DREAM!
MY DESTINY!

Contents

A Journey of a Thousand Miles Begins with a Single Step

Lao-Tzu

The Way of Lao-Tzu
Chinese Philosopher (604 BC-531 BC)

Chapter 1
Take Control of Your Time

Time Works For and Against Us
Depending Upon How We Use It

Israeli Prime Minister David Ben Gurion

Chapter 1

Take Control of Your Time

Tools of the Trade
SMARTGRADES HOMEWORK ACTION PLANNER

Steps to Success

Step 1. Write the words **Daily Action Plan** at top of page.

Step 2. Write a **To Do List** of a big goal and small steps.

Step 3. **Set Your Priorities:** Urgent, Important, Low, and Optional.

Step 4. **Divide and Conquer:** Break down big tasks into smaller more manageable tasks.

Step 5. Use Time Logs: **Estimated Time** and **Actual Time.**

Step 6. Life is a bumpy road lined with speedbumps. Make time for delays, detours, and distractions.

Step 7. Use checkboxes to keep track of completed tasks.

Step 8. Don't leave home without your **To Do List.**

Step 9. At the end of each day, review your game plan and refine it. Pay attention to strengths and weaknesses.

Step 10. Celebrate a job well done with a daily reward.

Plan Your Work and Work Your Plan

Don't Wish For It, Work For It

Success Comes in Cans, Not Cants

Well Done Is Better Than Well Said

The Only Something You Get for Nothing Is Failure

When You Lose, Don't Lose the Lesson

Step 1: Write a Daily Action Plan

Eat Right for the Energy to Learn:
Breakfast: Lunch: Dinner:

Daily Budget: $
Expense 1. $ Expense 2. $ Expense 3. $
Total Daily Expenses: $

Classes:
Subject: Time: Room:
Subject: Time: Room:

Study Period 1: (45 minutes each with 15 minute breaks)
Time: Study Area:
❑ Eat study snacks to stay energized, e.g., bananas and oranges
❑ Read class notes, handouts, and textbook
❑ Write Test Review Notes: Use **SMARTGRADES SUCCESS STRATEGY**

Daily Exercise Routine: Stretch, Aerobics, Weights, Stretch

Study Period 2: (45 minutes each with 15 minute breaks)
❑ Seek approval from teacher for outline of paper
❑ Preread tomorrow's chapter to prepare for class

Read a Daily Funny for Stress-Relief: "HA, HA, HA"

Part-Time Job:

Family Chores:

Social Life:

Regular Bedtime: 10 p.m.   Actual Bedtime:

Daily Reward for a Job Well Done:

Best Part of Day:

Worst Part of Day: Speedbumps; Delays, Detours, and Distractions

Step 2: Write a "To Do List"

Dreams Are Goals with Deadlines

Your **To Do List** consists of two kinds of lists, namely, the big picture or big idea, and the myriad of details.

TO DO LIST

BIG PICTURE
MANY DETAILS

For example, if you are going to the gym, your **To Do List** will probably look a lot like this one.

To Do List

Big Picture: Go to Gym: 1-2 p.m.

Many Details
- ☐ 1. Membership I.D.
- ☐ 2. Water bottle to stay hydrated
- ☐ 3. Weight lifting belt and gloves
- ☐ 4. iPod, headphones, check battery
- ☐ 5. Bring towel, shampoo, and comb
- ☐ 6. Vaseline and baby powder to reduce feet friction
- ☐ 7. Knee support brace

Step 3: Set Priorities
Urgent, Important, Low, and Optional

Write a **To Do List** that includes the big picture and the myriad of details, and assign one of the priorities below to each task.

Urgent

Cannot be postponed, immediate or emergency

Important

Needs attention today, but is not an emergency

Low

Can be put off until later in the week

Optional

Can be crossed off the list or postponed indefinately

For example, here are a list of tasks that need to be completed after school:

To Do List

☐ 1. Walk dog

☐ 2. Write English essay due tomorrow

☐ 3. Pick up groceries for dinner

☐ 4. Mail letter at post office

☐ 5. Buy fresh flowers for dinner table

Set Priorities

Prioritize the tasks by writing down one of the words from the list on the previous page.

To Do List

☐ 1. Walk dog: **URGENT**

☐ 2. Write English essay due tomorrow: **URGENT**

☐ 3. Pick up groceries for dinner: **IMPORTANT**

☐ 4. Mail a letter at post office: **LOW**

☐ 5. Buy fresh flowers for dinner table: **OPTIONAL**

URGENT: The dog has to be walked and the English essay has to be written today. Let's see how many tasks we can complete by spending a few minutes analyzing the list.

Choice 1: What if we walk the dog in the direction of the post office and mail the letter, and then on the way back from the post office, we walk by the florist and pick up some flowers for the dinner table.

To Do List

- ☐ 1. Walk dog: **URGENT**
- ☐ 2. Mail letter at post office: **LOW**
- ☐ 3. Buy fresh flowers for dinner table: **OPTIONAL**
- ☐ 4. Write English essay due tomorrow: **IMPORTANT**

Choice 2: Or we can walk the dog and mail the letter tomorrow and cross the flowers off the list for today. We have to bring the dog home before we can go to the store and pick up groceries or call a take-out restaurant for a delivery.

To Do List

- ☐ 1. Walk dog: **URGENT**
- ☐ 2. Pick up groceries for dinner: **IMPORTANT**
- ☐ 3. Write English essay due tomorrow: **URGENT**

DAILY ACTION PLAN

Make a detailed **To Do List** and set your priorities to meet your **URGENT** and **IMPORTANT** deadlines. If you can squeeze in the **LOW** and **OPTIONAL** tasks, then do so. If not, postpone them or cross them off the list.

Step 4: Divide and Conquer

Break Down Big Tasks into Smaller More Manageable Tasks

Most tasks have many steps. Each step takes a different amount of time to do. Some tasks appear overwhelming. When that happens, procrastination sets in. We can't seem to get started because the task requires too many steps, and there are many speed bumps along the way.

To Do List

Step 1. Write down the GOAL

Step 2. Write down STEPS required to achieve GOAL

Step 3. Set your priorities: URGENT, IMPORTANT, LOW

Step 4. Keep breaking down big tasks into smaller tasks

For example, I want to go to the gym to exercise. There are many steps involved. Here is my **To Do List** of the tasks that need to be accomplished before I can exercise.

To Do List: Join a Gym

- ☐ Priority 1. Purchase a gym membership
- ☐ Priority 2. Purchase a workout outfit and sneakers
- ☐ Priority 3. Purchase digital music
- ☐ Priority 4. Download music into cellphone

- ☐ Priority 5. Purchase book containing workout routines
- ☐ Priority 6. Purchase water bottle to stay hydrated
- ☐ Priority 7. Purchase gym bag to hold water bottle, exercise book, keys, I.D., and towel
- ☐ Priority 8. Go to gym to exercise

You will have to make another **To Do List** of exercises to get you into great shape, as follows:

To Do List: My Workout Routine

- ☐ Step 1. Stretch for 10 minutes to warm-up
- ☐ Step 2. Ride stationary bike for 15 minutes
- ☐ Step 3. Run on treadmill for 15 minutes
- ☐ Step 4. Do 25 sit-ups
- ☐ Step 5. Use weight machines for 30 minutes
- ☐ Step 6. Stretch for 10 minutes to cool down

You may decide that going to the gym is too complicated a task, and that you would rather take a half hour walk or ride your bicycle to get some aerobic activity and keep your heart in great shape.

To Do List: Ride Bike Around Park

- ☐ Step 1. Check air in tires
- ☐ Step 2. Check brakes
- ☐ Step 3. Stay hydrated, bring water bottle and snack
- ☐ Step 4. Ride bike along trail in park for one mile

Divide and Conquer: Every task needs to be broken down into smaller tasks, to make them more manageable and easier to complete. Let's take a closer look at each of the goals featured below.

Main Goal 1. Purchase Gym Membership

Divide and Conquer:

- ☐ 1. Call and make an appointment to speak to an agent
- ☐ 2. Meet with agent and take a tour of gym
- ☐ 3. Sign contract and pay with credit card/cash
- ☐ 4. Comb hair and prepare for photograph
- ☐ 5. Pose for photograph for a membership I.D.

Main Goal 2. Purchase workout outfit

Divide and Conquer:

- ☐ 1. Go to store and look for workout outfit
- ☐ 2. Try on outfit to see how it fits
- ☐ 3. Look for another outfit that fits better
- ☐ 4. Try on different outfits to find the best fit
- ☐ 5. Stand on a long checkout line to purchase outfit
- ☐ 6. Find new shelf space for outfit in cluttered closet

Main Goal 3. Purchase digital music to stay motivated

Divide and Conquer:

- ☐ 1. Go online and explore different kinds of music
- ☐ 2. Choose upbeat motivational artists and songs
- ☐ 3. Download music into cellphone

For Example: Write a School Paper

Your teacher will either assign an essay or a research paper, and each academic task needs to be broken down into smaller more manageable tasks, as follows:

Big Task: Write an English essay for class on abortion

Divide and Conquer:

☐ Step 1. Use encyclopedia for general overview of topic.

☐ Step 2. Read bibliographic citations to find experts in field and primary and secondary source materials.

☐ Step 3. Read primary sources for pro and con arguments.

☐ Step 4. Choose a position and write a thesis statement.

☐ Step 5. Write outline of main ideas and supporting examples.

☐ Step 6. Use outline to write rough draft of paper.

Divide and Conquer: Always break down big tasks that appear to be overwhelming into smaller tasks that are easier to navigate. This is the antidote for bouts of procrastination that can paralyze and cripple productivity, and derail academic success.

Step 5. Use Time Logs

Write down"Estimated" and "Actual" Time

To take control of your time, you have to write down two different measurements:

Estimated Time (Fantasy)   Actual Time (Reality)

Estimated Time (Fantasy, Wishful Thinking)
The first amount of time is the estimated time. This is the time you would like the task to take. This time is usually a miscalculation because of the speedbumps.

Actual Time (Time Plus Life's Inevitable Setbacks)
The second amount of time is the actual time. Most tasks will take longer to accomplish because life is a bumpy road of setbacks (this is normal). In "REAL LIFE" there are many speed bumps called delays, detours, and distractions that will slow you down and get in your way.

For example: Write a Research Paper

Step 1. Choose a topic and title   1/2 Hour
Step 2. Do research   5 Hours
Step 3. Write outline   1 Hour
Step 4. Write rough and final draft   10 Hours
Step 5. Proofread paper to perfection   2 Hours

Time Log
Estimated Time: 18 1/2 Hours
Actual Time: 20 1/2 Hours
Error: 2 hours (trip to store, no ink, out of paper)

Delay: My printer ran out of ink and I had to stop at the store to pick up a new cartridge.

Detour: The store was closed and I had to wait until the next day to pick up the ink to print out my paper.

Distraction: On the way to the store, I passed my favorite pizza shop and decided to grab a quick slice.

On one hand, your class time and test time are easy to manage because they have fixed times:

Go to class: 1 hour per class (fixed)   Actual Time
Take a test: 1 hour per test (fixed)   Actual Time

On the other hand, your study schedule will be difficult to manage because different assignments take different amounts of time to complete. Your assignments have variable times, as folllows:

Academic Assignments:

1. End of Chapter Questions   2-3 Hours (variable)
2. English Essay   5-10 Hours (variable)
3. Research Report   10-25 Hours (variable)
4. Test Preparation   5-25 Hours (variable)

Let's apply our **SMARTGRADES** Time Management Tools to our English essay assignment, as follows:

First: We create a **"To Do List"** (big picture and details).
Second: We set priorities: urgent, important, and low.
Third: We break down the big task into smaller tasks.
Fourth: We add estimated and actual time logs.
Fifth: We record speedbumps: delays, detours, and distractions.
Sixth: We use checkboxes for completed tasks.
Seventh: We celebrate a job well done with a reward.

Big Academic Task

Write a 5 page English essay

Steps to Success

☐ Step 1. Use encyclopedia for general overview of topic
Time Log
Estimated Time: 1 Hour
Actual Time:
Speedbumps: Any Delays, Detours, and Distractions?

____

☐ Step 2. Read bibliographic citations for experts in field and primary and secondary source materials
Time Log
Estimated Time: 45 Minutes
Actual Time:
Speedbumps: Any Delays, Detours, and Distractions?

____

☐ Step 3. Read primary sources for pro and con arguments
Time Log
Estimated Time: 5 Hours
Actual Time:
Speedbumps: Any Delays, Detours, and Distractions?

☐ Step 4. Write outline of main ideas and supporting details
Time Log
Estimated Time: 3 Hours
Actual Time:
Speedbumps: Any Delays, Detours, and Distractions?

____

☐ Step 5. Meet with teacher for approval of outline
Time Log
Estimated Time: 1/2 Hour
Actual Time:
Speedbumps: Any Delays, Detours, and Distractions?

____

☐ Step 6. Use outline to write rough draft of paper
Time Log
Estimated Time: 10 Hours
Actual Time:
Speedbumps: Any Delays, Detours, and Distractions?

____

☐ Step 7. Meet with teacher for approval of rough draft
Time Log
Estimated Time: 1 Hour
Actual Time:
Speedbumps: Any Delays, Detours, and Distractions?

____

☐ Step 8. Write final draft and proofread to perfection
Time Log
Estimated Time: 10 Hours
Actual Time:
Speedbumps: Any Delays, Detours, and Distractions?

____☐

Step 9. Hand in paper and earn an A grade. Celebrate.

Step 6. Setbacks
Life Is a Bumpy Road of
Delays, Detours, and Distractions

Setbacks are inevitable. There are many different types of setbacks. Life is a bumpy road of delays, detours, and distractions that have to be anticipated and calculated.

Delays: You keep miscalculating the "Real Time" it takes to complete a goal.

Detours: You are supposed to go to the tutoring center to ask for help, but your friend calls and invites you to a game.

Distractions: You are looking for one article on the internet but find yourself distracted by tabloid gossip.

At the end of each day, look at your **Daily Action Plan** and see what is working and what is not working.

Q. What types of **delays** are taking your time?

A. The subway is faster than the bus or taxi due to traffic

Q. What types of **detours** are taking your time?

A. Spending too much time socializing with friends

Q. What types of **distractions** are taking your time?

A. I am watching too many reality TV shows on weeknights

Less is More Is One Key to Success

Doing less is a good idea. Don't try to squeeze too many activities into one day. Spread your activities over a longer period of time. Instead of thinking daily, think weekly, monthly, or yearly for some of the things you want to accomplish. Take baby steps each and every day toward a goal that you will reach by the end of the year.

- Daily Test Review Notes: **SMARTGRADES SUCCESS STRATEGY**
- Exercise three times a week
- Have dinner with family once a week
- Go to a sporting event once a month
- Visit museum exhibit every six months

Simplicity is One Key to Success

Keep each day as simple as possible. Streamline your life for simplicity. Simplicity is making a **"Daily Action Plan"** that contains only life's necessities.

- ☐ 1. Eat Right for Energy to Learn (whole grains)
- ☐ 2. Sleep Well for Energy to Learn (8 Hours)
- ☐ 3. Exercise for Energy to Learn (1/2 Hr. walk)
- ☐ 4. Go to Class and then Write a Test Review Note
- ☐ 5. Ace Tests with Your **SMARTGRADES SUCCESS STRATEGY**
- ☐ 6. Call Home: **"Mom, I Earned an A Grade Today"**
- ☐ 7. Celebrate Success with a Reward for a Job Well Done

Let's Recap: How to Take Control of Your Time

1. Write a To Do List of the Big Picture and Add Details

Big Picture: Write an English Essay

1. Choose a Researchable Topic

2. Do Research

3. Write Outline

4. Write a Rough and Final Draft

5. Proofread to Perfection

----

2. Set Your Priorities:

1. Urgent (Do Now)

2. Important (Do Today)

3. Low (Leave for Another Day)

4. Optional (Cross off List)

----

3. Divide and Conquer: Breakdown Big Task -> Smaller Tasks

1. Choose Topic

a. Choose a topic that is researchable

2. Research Topic

a. Use encyclopedia for a general overview of topic

b. Read for experts in the field

c. Read for pro and con arguments

d. Read bibliographic citations for primary source materials

3. Write an Outline

a. List the main ideas and supporting pro and con arguments

4. Write Down Time Logs: Estimated and Actual Time

☐ Step 1. Read encyclopedia for experts in field
Estimated Time: 1 Hour
Actual Time:
Error Time:
Speedbumps: Any Delays, Detours, and Distractions?

☐ Step 2. Read the primary source material
Estimated Time: 5 Hours
Actual Time:
Error Time:
Speedbumps: Any Delays, Detours, and Distractions?

☐ Step 3. Make a list of pro and con arguments
Estimated Time: 3 Hours
Actual Time:
Error Time:
Speedbumps: Any Delays, Detours, and Distractions?

5. Use Checkboxes to Keep Track of Completed Tasks

☐ 1.   ☐ 2.

6. Review Your Game Plan and Refine it. Pay Attention to Your Strengths and Weaknesses.

Strength: Right after class, I wrote Test Review Notes

Weakness: Wasted 2 hours on internet tabloid gossip

Step 7: Celebrate a Job Well Done with a Daily Reward

Today's Reward: Movie night

Mile by Mile, Life's a Trial.
Yard by Yard, It's Not So Hard.
Inch by Inch, It's a Cinch

Chapter 2
Multiple Schedules
Make Big Plans and Take Small Steps

The Key is Not to Prioritize What's on Your
Schedule, But to Schedule Your Priorities

Stephen Covey

Chapter 2
Multiple Schedules
Make Big Plans and Take Small Steps

Your life will revolve around ten different types of schedules and you will need to write them down, analyze them, and reconfigure them, so that there is a seamless flow between them, instead of conflict, confusion, and chaos.

Schedule 1. Eat Right for Energy to Learn (variable)

Schedule 2. Class Schedule (fixed)

Schedule 3. Study Schedule (variable)

Schedule 4. Test Schedule (fixed)

Schedule 5. Exercise Schedule (variable)

Schedule 6. Part-Time Job Schedule (fixed)

Schedule 7. Family Chores Schedule (variable)

Schedule 8. Social Life Schedule (variable)

Schedule 9. Extra-Curricular School Activities (variable)

Schedule 10. Free Time (variable and negligible)

My Multiple Schedules Worksheet

Schedule 1. Eat Right for the Energy to Learn (variable)
M: Whole grains, protein, fresh fruits and vegetables
T:
W:
T:
F:
S: Nibbled on junk food at birthday party
S: Back on track: Ditto

Schedule 2. Class Schedule (fixed)

M:

T:

W:

T:

F:

Schedule 3. Study Periods (variable)
M: Right after class, write your Test Review Notes
T:
W:
T:
F:
S: **Rest, Relaxation, and Recovery**
S: Write "Daily Action Plan" for next week

Schedule 4. Test Schedule (fixed)

Schedule 5. Exercise (variable)
M: Go to school gym to lift weights
T: Ride bicycle in park
W: **Rest, Relaxation, and Recovery**
T: Go to school gym to lift weights
F: Swim in school pool
S: **Rest, Relaxation, and Recovery**
S: Jog around school track

Schedule 6. Part Time Job (fixed)
M:
T:
W:
T:
F:
S: Dog walker for ten dogs (2 HRS., $5/HR. = $100)
S:

Schedule 7. Family Responsibilities (variable)
M:
T:
W:
T:
F:
S:
S: Clean cat litter, do laundry, mow lawn

Schedule 8. Extra-Curricular Activities (fixed)
M:
T: Volunteer to feed homeless, 4-5 p.m.
W:
T: Join ball room dance club, 7-8 p.m. (met sweetheart)
F:
S:
S:

Schedule 9. Social Life Schedule (variable)
M: School night
T: School night
W: School night
T: School night
F: Friday night is for friends
S: Saturday night is date night
S:

Schedule 10. Free Time Schedule (variable and negligible)

Take Control of Your Social Life Schedule

Keeping in touch with friends takes time. Pick a time to chat with your friends. Don't answer the phone and interrupt your study period every time a friend calls to talk with you, unless that friend is your study buddy. Pick a time after your school work is completed to make your social calls and stay connected to your loved ones.

Examples:

1. Suzy called about making a plan for Friday night

Action Plan: Call her back at 9:30 p.m.

Time Log

Estimated Time: 10 Minutes

Actual Time: 1 1/2 Hours

Error: 1 Hour and 20 Minutes

Delays, Detours, and Distractions: Gossiping

Action Plan: Friday, 8 P.M. for movie, meet at cafe

2. Peter called to have dinner on Saturday, date night

Action Plan: Call him back at 7:45 p.m.

Time Log

Estimated Time:

Actual Time:

Error:

Delays, Detours, and Distractions:

Action Plan: Saturday, 7 p.m., he will pick me up

My Social Life Schedule (Variable)

Making new friends and keeping in touch with old friends takes time. Your friends will change over time and place.

Q: How often do you introduce yourself to a new person?
a. Daily   b. Weekly   c. Monthly   d. Yearly

Here's how to introduce yourself to a new person:
1. Smile and make eye contact.
2. Say "Hello."
3. Ask a simple question? "What time do you have?"
4. Offer a compliment: "I love your blue sweater."
5. Introduce yourself: "My name is . . ."
6. What's your name?
7. Find common ground:
a. New study buddy
b. New girlfriend or boyfriend
c. New teammate for sports
d. New business partner for start-up internet business

Great relationships are based on connection, chemistry, compatibility, caring, communication, companionship, and common ground. When you meet someone, take notes:
Q1. What kind of connection do we have?
Q2. Do we have chemistry?
Q3. Are we compatible?
Q4. Is there genuine affection between us?
Q5. Do we have common interests?
Q6. Do we have honest communication?

Crash Course on Relationships for the 21st Century

Strengths and Weaknesses

Relationships are difficult because every person in your life will help you with their strengths and hurt you with their weaknesses. There is no exception to this rule.

Unconditional and Conditional Love

Adult relationships are based on conditional love. Most of the time, people don't love you, they only love what they want from you. Unconditional love is given only by your parents and pets.

You Don't Find Love, You Create Love

Love is not a natural resource. Love is an artificial construction comprised of mutual respect and admiration. For a connection to occur, you have to be on a similar frequency. On a daily basis, for love to exist, you have to bring love into your life.

Self-Love Is True Love

You have to stay true to yourself and your own dreams. No one in your life will ever be as good to you as you are to yourself, because only you will ever know yourself and understand your own needs. Most people do not have enough love inside of them to do what they need to do for themselves, let alone to love you.

Relationships Are Bonus Love

If you find a loving relationship with someone besides yourself, that love is called "Bonus Love." Bonus Love is is "extra love" that adds more love to the foundation of love that you create and recreate on a daily basis for yourself.

A Friend Walks In When Everyone Else Walks Out

APRIL 30
Poetry In Your Pocket Day

TRUE LOVE

True Love is Unconditional.
True Love is Found in the Deed.
True Love is Found in the We.
True Love Unites the Mind,
Body, and Heart as One.

Sharon Esther Lampert
© All Rights Reserved.

Place this poem into your pocket
and the positive vibrational energy
will bring TRUE LOVE into your life.

www.WorldFamousPoems.com
The Greatest Poems Ever Written on Extraordinary World Events

The Sole Intention of My Poetry Is to Add **LIGHT** to Your So

APRIL 30
Poetry In Your Pocket Day

IMPOSSIBLE

It is impossible to breathe in air,
Without breathing in toxic pollutants.

It is impossible to ingest nutritious food,
Without ingesting chemicals and preservatives.

It is impossible to have a loving relationship,
Without bumping into a loved one's
emotional problems.

And it is impossible not to breathe, eat, and love.

Sharon Esther Lampert

SEE THE WORLD THROUGH THE EYES OF A CREATIVE GENIUS
© All Rights Reserved.

www.PoetryJewels.com
Diamonds, Emeralds, Sapphires, Rubies, and Pearls

The Sole Intention of My Poetry Is to Add **LIGHT** to Your Soul

APRIL 30
Poetry In Your Pocket Day

FINITE

Days Live and Die.
Suns Rise and Set.
Flowers Bloom and Wither.
Fruits Ripen and Spoil.
Ice Cream Freezes and Melts.
Candles Shed Light and Darken.
Energies Are Generated and Depleted.
Monies Are Made and Spent.
Time Is Used and Squandered.
Love Burns Eternal and Passions Wane.
Lives Are Breathed and Become Breathless.

Sharon Esther Lampert

© All Rights Reserved.

www.WorldFamousPoems.com
The Greatest Poems Ever Written on Extraordinary World Events

The Sole Intention of My Poetry Is to Add **LIGHT** to Your Soul

APRIL 30
Poetry In Your Pocket Day

What Other People Think

People who want to like you
will find something to like about you.
These people are called your **FRIENDS**.

People who don't want to like you
will find something not to like about you.
These people are called your **CRITICS**.

People who don't want to like you
but can't find something about you
not to like will make something up.
These people are called your **ENEMIES**.

Sharon Esther Lampert

© All Rights Reserved.

www.WorldFamousPoems.com
The Greatest Poems Ever Written on Extraordinary World Events

The Sole Intention of My Poetry Is to Add **LIGHT** to Your Soul

The Energy of the Mind
Is the Essence of Life

Aristotle
Ancient Greek Philosopher, Scientist, and Physician
384 BC-322 BC

Chapter 3
Eat Right for the Energy to Learn, Laugh, and Love

Q: Are You Hungry for the Energy to Learn?
Whole Grain High Fiber Breakfast
Power Lunch: (Big Plate)
Lite Dinner: (Small Plate)
Power Study Snacks

Chapter 3
Eat for Energy to Learn, Laugh, and Love

Q1. What Did You Eat this Morning?

You can't learn on an empty stomach. It takes energy to learn. Energy comes from good nutrition and sufficient sleep. First you feed your body with food, and then you feed your mind with facts.

Your electrical appliances will not work without a boost of electricity, and your brain will not work without a boost of whole grain fiber, protein, fresh fruits and vegetables loaded with natural (not synthetic) vitamins and minerals.

Think of yourself as a car with a gas tank that has to be filled up to be able to take you places. First, you fill your tank and then you drive. First, you eat a nutritious meal and then you go to school to learn. If you don't eat properly, your brain will not have the "FULL GAS TANK" to be able to read, think, question, research, write, memorize, and test.

Q2. Did You Put Some Love Into It?

Learning requires love. You have to put love into everything that you do. Your heart and your mind have to be working together as a team. According to the poet, philosopher, and educator, Sharon Esther Lampert, "You don't find love, you create love." Love has to be created. Like a warm and cozy fire on a cold winter's night, you have to create love for it to exist in the world.

Q3. Did You Laugh Today?

Learning requires a sense of humor. The learning curve is steep. It takes time to learn. Learning requires trial'n'error. Learning requires patience and practice until mastery is achieved. Sometimes you will have to get it all wrong, before you can get it all right. It is best to not take yourself so seriously, and to learn to laugh at yourself from time to time as you will often stumble blindly in the dark trying to figure out what your strengths and weaknesses are, where you belong in the world, and how you can make a difference and, ultimately, a contribution of meaningful significance.

Try not to let a day go by without a laugh that will bring a smile to your face. Late night TV talk shows use the daily newspaper as a spring board for spinning human trials and tribulations into comedy. The day may start out bleakly, but it always ends with a laugh. But don't stay up late to watch these TV shows, rather watch the reruns on the internet the next day, and go to bed at a decent hour. Almost every TV show is recorded on the internet, so you can watch them at your convenience, when you need a study break and a good laugh.

The Best Study Break Is the Website T.E.D.

T.E.D. is a website showcasing interesting people in the world, who make a difference. These people are hardly ever featured on TV. These people will inspire you, as you embark on your own academic journey in search of a purpose in life that is imbued with passion and prosperity.

Change Your Knowledge Base

Quite often, you will have to change your "Knowledge Base." To move forward in the world, you will have to leave the past behind, and get on a new road that will take you to a new place that is entirely different from where you came from and what you were taught.

Old Knowledge Base: "I can eat anything I want, as long as I eat in moderation."

New Knowledge Base: "I can't eat anything I want because the processed food is loaded with salt, sugar, corn syrup, and a whole host of chemicals and preservatives that I can't pronounce, spell, or remember.

Here are a few of the consequences of eating processed food:

- My body will not have sufficient vitamins and minerals

- I will always feel tired and want to eat more junk

- My body will overeat processed food trying to get energy from the food

- I will become overweight and undernourished

New Knowledge Base: Avoid Processed Food

I will not eat anything wrapped in plastic that can live for more than ten years in my knapsack, including those packaged protein bars (loaded with sugar).

How to Eat Right for the Energy to Learn

You are a biological machine that needs fiber fuel to be able to think, read, research, write, memorize, and test. Before you leave for school, you need to have a system in place to manage your energy needs.

The Fiber Facts
Whole Grain Foods = Long-Term Energy and No Cravings

My 30-Second Breakfast

- Grab a bran muffin (try a different flavor each day)
- Grab two hard-boiled eggs (protein)
- Grab fruit: banana, apple, and orange (vitamins)
- Grab a container of orange juice (hydration)

My One-Minute Breakfast

- A slice of whole grain toast, cheese, tomato (fiber)
- Grab two hard-boiled eggs (protein)
- Grab fruit: banana, apple, and orange (vitamins)
- Grab a container of orange juice (hydration)

My Five-Minute Breakfast (Breakfast of Champions)

- A bowl of delicious and creamy oatmeal, add walnuts, sliced banana, cinnamon, and maple syrup. Drink a glass of orange juice.

My Power Lunch (Big Plate)

Fill big plate with 1/4 fist-sized protein and 3/4 vegetables
Monday: Fish with spinach, carrots, grilled red peppers
Tuesday: Meat with broccoli, carrots, corn
Wednesday: Fish with spinach, carrots, cauliflower
Thursday: Meat with green beans, carrots, corn
Friday: Fish with spinach, carrots, grilled red pepper

My Lite Dinner (Small Plate)

Fill small plate with 1/4 fist-sized protein and 3/4 vegetables
1. Eat off of a small plate to reduce your portion size
2. Eat dinner before 7 P.M.
3. Fill up on salad, vegetable soup, steamed vegetables
4. Avoid fried, fatty, and greasy food
5. Avoid heavy foods that put you to sleep after a meal
6. Avoid foods with sugar that keep you up late at night
7. No caffeinated drinks after 5 P.M. (poor sleep)

My Power Study Snacks for the Energy to Learn

1. Golden delicious apples with peanut butter or cheese
2. Fresh berries with yogurt and nuts, add honey
3. Carrot and celery sticks with humus
4. Bran muffins (cranberry, banana, carrot, apple)

EVERY DAY AN EASY A

Make Your Own Food Plan for the Energy to Learn

My 30-Second Breakfast

Whole Grain Fiber (long lasting fuel, no cravings):

____

Protein: _______________________________

Vegetables: _______________________________

Fruits: _______________________________

Hydration (sugar free): _________________________

My One-Minute Breakfast

Whole Grain Fiber (long lasting fuel, no cravings):

____

Protein: _______________________________

Vegetables: _______________________________

Fruits: _______________________________

Hydration (sugar free): _________________________

My Five-Minute Breakfast

Whole Grain Fiber (long lasting fuel, no cravings):

____

Protein: _______________________________

Vegetables: _______________________________

Fruits: _______________________________

Hydration (sugar free): _________________________

My Power Lunch (Big Plate)

Protein: Fish/Meat/Beans ________________________________

Vegetables: ________________________________

Fruits: ________________________________

Hydration (sugar free): ________________________________

Low Fat Dessert: ________________________________

My Lite Dinner (Small Plate for Small Portions)

Protein: Fish/Meat/Bean ________________________________

Vegetables: ________________________________

Fruits: ________________________________

Hydration (sugar free): ________________________________

Low Fat Dessert: ________________________________

No Caffeine After 5 P.M. (poor sleep, tired next day)

My Power Study Snacks for the Energy to Learn

Monday: ________________________________

Tuesday: ________________________________

Wednesday: ________________________________

Thursday: ________________________________

Friday: ________________________________

Saturday: ________________________________

Sunday: ________________________________

A Place for Everything, Everything in its Place

Benjamin Franklin

Chapter 4
Organize the Mountain of Academic Materials

Don't Agonize, Organize!
Florynce R. Kennedy

Chapter 4

Take Control of the Facts

Organize Your Academic Materials

Take control of the facts. School is a game of facts.
Your job is to **RETRIEVE** the facts and **RETURN** the facts.
First, you will retrieve the facts from the blackboard (class
notes), handouts, and textbook, and then you will return
the facts to the teacher in an essay, research paper, and on
a test. You need to have an organization system in place to
manage the voluminous academic facts.

For Example
Class: English
The academic facts come from 3 sources:
1. Class notes
2. Handouts
3. Textbook

For each set of facts, you will write Test Review Notes.
You will now have 3 sets of Test Review Notes:
1. Class notes + Test Review Notes
2. Handouts   + Test Review Notes
3. Textbook   + Test Review Notes
4. Homework Assignments, Quizzes, and Tests

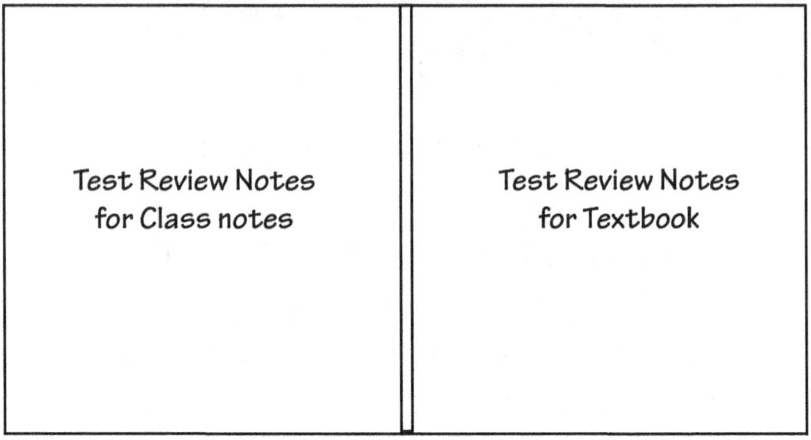

Test Review Notes
for Class notes

Test Review Notes
for Textbook

Blue Folder 1/English

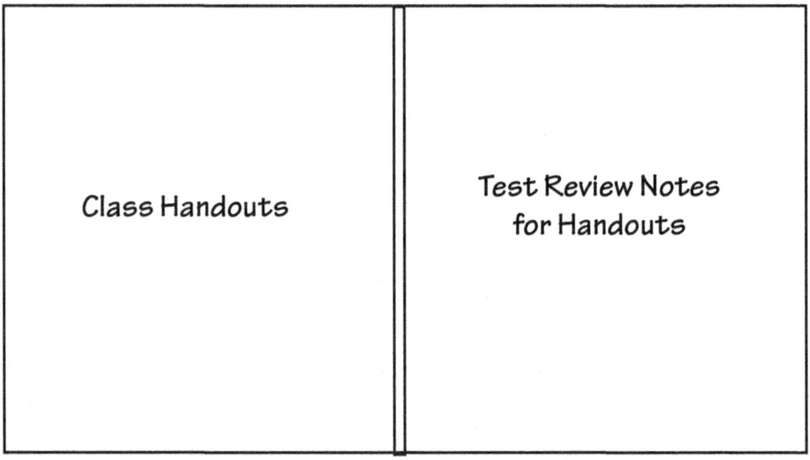

Class Handouts

Test Review Notes
for Handouts

Blue Folder 2/English

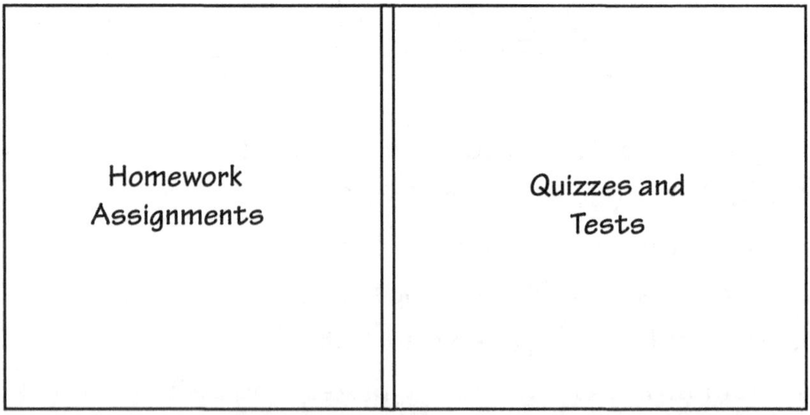

Homework
Assignments

Quizzes and
Tests

Blue Folder 3/English

Option 1. Cheap School Notebooks & Color-Coded Folders

Buy a school notebook for each class and buy color-coded folders to keep track of the following:

1. Test Review Notes (class notes, handouts, and textbook)
2. Quizzes
3. Tests
4. Homework Assignments

Buy Color-Coded Folders for Each Class:

English   Blue Folder
Math   Green Folder
Science   Yellow Folder
History   Purple Folder
Language   Red Folder

Label Your Blue Folders (3 Folders Per Class)
Folder 1. Test Review Notes
Pocket 1. Class Notes Test Review Notes
Pocket 2. Textbook Test Review Notes

Folder 2. Class Handouts
Pocket 1. Handouts
Pocket 2. Test Review Notes for Handouts

Folder 3. Homework, Quizzes, and Tests
Pocket 1. Homework Assignments
Pocket 2. Quizzes and Tests

SMARTGRADES
School Notebooks

Good Grades Become Grand Dreams

www.smartgrades.com

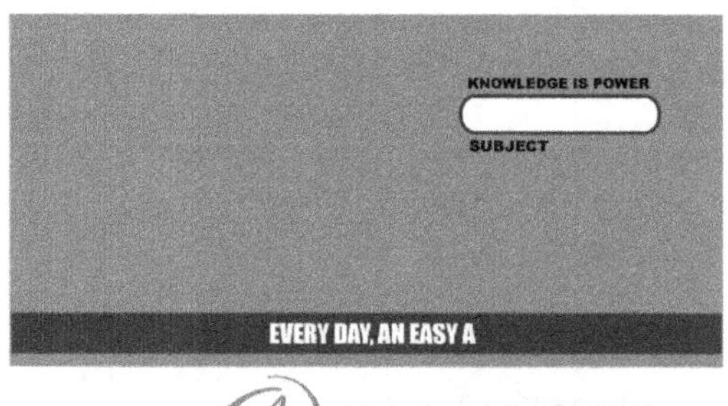

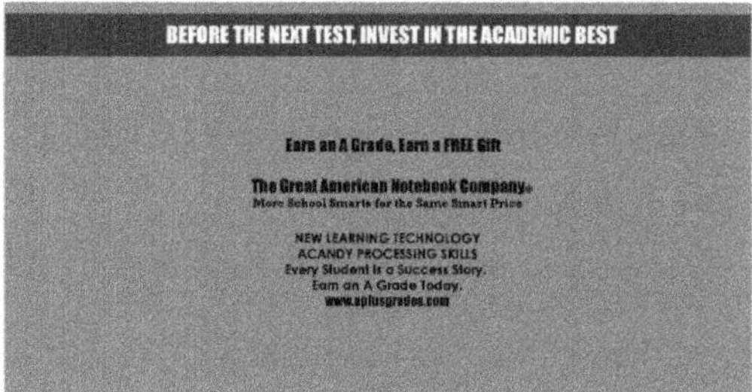

THE ESSENTIALS

Class Notes and Test-Review Notes in One Notebook
- How to Ace Every Test Every Time
- How to Ace a Multiple Choice Test
- How to Ace an Essay Test
- How to Write a Research Paper
- Homework Action Planner

Option 2. SMARTGRADES SCHOOL NOTEBOOKS
You can take class notes and write Test Review Notes in the same notebook, and the new learning technology, **SMARTGRADES SUCCESS STRATEGY** are at your fingertips. There is also a notebook for textbook Test Review Notes and research papers.

Buy Homework Action Planner
SMARTGRADES Homeowork Action Planner organizes your life

Notebook 1. Class Notes and Test Review Notes
SMARTGRADES School Notebook for Class Notes and Test Review Notes

Notebook 2. Textbook Test Review Notes
SMARTGRADES School Notebook for Textbook Test Review Notes

Notebook 3. Research Papers
SMARTGRADES Research School Notebook

Handouts and Test-Review Notes
One color-coded folder for handouts and Test Review Notes

Homework, Quizzes, and Tests
One color-coded folder for homework, quizzes, and tests

SMARTGRADES Advantage
- Buy a **SMARTGRADES** School Notebook and keep the receipt

- **SMARTGRADES** Learning Tools at Your Fingertips

- Earn A Grades, Earn FREE Gift!
  (mail in receipt as proof of purchase)

- **PHOTON SUPERHERO of EDUCATION** will call you to congratulate you on your academic success.

How to Organize Your Study Area

Tools of the Trade

Choose a Great Study Area
Choose a Power Study Snack
Buy, Rent, or Borrow Textbooks
Choose a School Library Locker

Steps to Success

Right after class, you will immediately go to your favorite study area and write your Test Review Notes. You will read your class notes, handout, and textbook and use your ten step **SMARTGRADES SUCCESS STRATEGY** for Instant & Total Recall to ace your tests (Chapter 7).

How to Choose a Great Study Area

☐ 1. Choose a study area with no external distractions

☐ 2. Spacious desk for notebook, textbook, and reference materials

☐ 3. Comfortable chair that fits your body type

☐ 4. Good lighting

☐ 5. Computer with internet connection, printer, ink, and paper

☐ 6. External hard drive for daily backups of schoolwork

☐ 7. Pens, pencils, stapler, tape, paper clips, and ruler

How to Choose a Power Study Snack

Learning requires a great deal of energy. Every two hours, you will need some nutrition. When you are hungry, you will start searching for food. You will waste a lot of time walking up and down the aisles of a supermarket, and will be tempted as a result of persuasive advertisements to choose some processed food in a plastic wrapper that is loaded with sugar and salt and is devoid of vitamins and minerals. Or you will succumb to eating greasy junk food that will leave you undernourished and fat.

On one hand, you may need that walk to stretch your legs and get some fresh air. On the other hand, there are too many temptations, and you will waste too much time and spend more money than your budget allows.

Make a Daily Power Study Snack Plan:

M: Yogurt, granola, and fruit

T: Bran muffin in a variety of flavors

W: Turkey sandwich with red peppers and cheese

TH: Carrots and celery sticks with humus

F: Trail Mix: Almonds, walnuts, cranberries, raisins

• Always carry a bottle of water with you to stay hydrated.

• Avoid soft drinks loaded with sugar that make you fat.

How to Buy, Rent, or Borrow Textbooks

☐ **Plan A.** Pay Full Price for Brand New Textbooks

Buy brand new textbooks at full price and later sell them to a used bookstore or to another student.

☐ **Plan B.** Pay Half Price for Used Textbooks

Buy textbooks at half-price by buying used textbooks. Checkout: Biblio.com, Abebooks.com, A1books.com, Maketextbooksaffordable.org, and Bookfinder.com.

☐ **Plan C.** Free Textbooks at the Library

Free copies of textbooks are in the school library.

☐ **Plan D.** Free Textbooks from My Friends

Students have used textbooks that they may give away for free because they are not in good shape.

☐ **Plan E.** Cheap Textbooks from My Friends

Students have used textbooks in good condition that they will be happy to sell for half price.

☐ **Plan F.** Share Textbooks with Your Study Buddy

If you are taking the same class with a good friend and study partner, buy one set of textbooks and share them.

How to Choose a School Library Locker

Lugging heavy textbooks is bad for your back and posture.

Q: Are you starting to slouch?

Most schools have lockers in the library. This is a great place for a locker because you can leave your heavy textbooks in your locker and study in the library. You won't have to carry heavy books back and forth from the library. You will also be able to place your supplementary library books into your locker.

First Come, First Serve
The top lockers are reserved early and first. If you wait too long to buy a library locker, you will have to buy a bottom locker that is adjacent to your knees.

To Do List: The School Library Locker

☐ 1. Call school library and ask if there are library lockers.

☐ 2. Go to the library and examine the lockers.

☐ 3. Pick a locker on the same floor as your major
    e.g., Major in Psychology, 4th Floor = Psych Books

☐ 4. Add your **SMARTGRADES** School Notebooks and textbooks to your locker. You can also add your gym clothes.

☐ 5. Checkout supplementary PSYCH textbooks that will help you learn the academic materials, and add to locker.

1. RECOGNIZE Your Star Qualities.

2. LISTEN to Your Inner Voice.

3. PROTECT Your Needs and Desires.

4. Have COURAGE to Abandon Relationships with insensitive people.

5. Attach Your HEART to Your HEAD and Make Decisions in Your Best Interest.

6. EMPOWER Yourself to Make the Necessary Changes to Ensure Your Happiness.

7. Have the VISION to See Beyond Present Difficulties and Create a Stress-Free Lifestyle.

8. Take Good Care of Yourself, You Belong to You

PHOTON
SUPERHERO OF EDUCATION
www.BooksnotBombs.com

Chapter 5
Manage Your Worry, Anxiety, Stress, and Bouts of Depression

If You Learn Anything at Cornell,
Please Learn to Ask for Help.
It is a Sign of Wisdom and Strength

David Skorton
President of Cornell University

2010: Six Student Suicides in Six Months

According to the Jed Foundation, it is
roughly estimated that 24,000 suicide
attempts and 1,100 suicides occur annually
among U.S. college students aged 18 to 24
years (The Jed Foundation, 2008).

Chapter 5
Manage Your Worry, Anxiety, Stress, and Bouts of Depression

Here are some of the reasons that most, if not all, students are anxious, stressed, and suffer "bouts of depression."

1. **Poor Time Management Tools:** Time cannot be saved. Students do not know how to take control of their time to make every hour count toward reaching their academic goals (Chapter 1 and 2).

2. **Disorganization:** The academic facts are voluminous (class notes, handouts, and textbook) and students do not have an organization system in place to manage the mountain of facts (Chapter 4).

3. **Energy Is Scattered in Too Many Directions:** Students are over scheduled. KEEP LIFE SIMPLE. Stick to your priorities of class, study period, part-time job, and exercise. Limit yourself to one or two activities a week, e.g., sporting event, music concert, or film.

4. **No Energy to Learn:** Students eat fast food, junk food and processed food devoid of nutrition (Chapter 3).

5. **Poor Processing Tools:** Students wait until the night before a test to start memorizing academic material. Students do not have learning tools to process the facts for long-term retention to ace their tests (Chapter 7).

6. **Financial Stress:** Students have not yet found their passion and purpose in life. Students are graduating with astronomical school loan debt and an insecure future.

7. **No Entrepreneurial Tools to Start Their Own Businesses:** Students are not required to take business classes, but 80% of all businesses are small businesses.

8. **Relationship Stress:** Students are trying to form an intimate attachment with a member of the opposite (or same) sex to form a partnership of mutual affection and admiration. Bonding your soul with the soul of another person for love, sex, and companionship is a challenging undertaking because both of you are still maturing and don't have defined identities. As a result, relationships are fragile. All breakups are painful to one degree or another.

9. **Worry, Anxiety, and Stress Can Escalate into Depression and Suicide:** Students feel overwhelmed by the demands of school, work, part-time jobs, and relationships (family, friends, and intimate partner). When disappointments build up, so does the emotional pain. The emotional pain can be too much to bear and depression will take hold of your soul and immobilize you.

LIFE IS UNFAIR

Everything Under the Sun Has a Short
Lifespan and an Expiration Date.

Disappointments Multiply –>
Emotional Pain Is Too Much To Bear –>
Pain –> Rage –> Depression –>Suicide

For Example: This Student Is Having a Bad Week

1. Unfair Tricky Test Questions –> Emotional Pain

A student is sabotaged by unfair tricky test questions from a teacher with an ax to grind. You paid your tuition, studied for hours, and the entire class fails the test and it is graded on a curve. This teacher is undermining your self-confidence, destroying your self-esteem, and your dream for the future. Tip: Get the inside scoop on the class, before you sign up for it.

2. Illness or Death in the Family —> Emotional Pain

The doctor did not diagnose the symptoms in time and now it is too late to help your family member. The bad news has broken your heart. Grieving the loss of a loved one takes at least three years.

3. Your Partner Breaks Up with You –> Emotional Pain

Your partner has been cheating on you and you find out by walking in on them accidentally. You are in a state of shock. This pain takes years to heal. You may even be scarred for life and unable to love again.

4. You Get Fired from Your Job –> Emotional Pain

Your boss doesn't care that your parent died and if you take the day off to go to the funeral, you're fired. You go to the funeral and start looking for a new job. You will completely recover from this kind of setback.

DO NOT START POPPING THOSE VACUOUS PILLS FOR DEPRESSION

WHY?

Because all medications have side effects and you will find that you will now be suffering from your emotional pain and from the side effects of these medications. These pills are also dangerous because when you feel emotional pain, you keep popping the pills, like candy, overdose, and die. Prescription drugs are more dangerous than illegal drugs. These pills mask your emotional pain, and will not help you to grieve your losses and heal.

FEEL TO HEAL

When you feel pain, go into a private area and cry out your emotional pain and grief for hours, weeks, days, or years. The loss of a loved one can evoke tears for years to come, and you need to let the pain rise to the surface and be released. The day will come when the grief is over, and you will regain your vitality and zest for life.

DO NOT GIVE YOUR POWER AWAY

Do not give your power away to the people who come into your life and cause you pain. Here is a mantra that will help you change course and keep you on track for personal and professional success in school and in the real world.

"The First Day It Is Crazy, Is The First Day That It Is Over"

Sharon Esther Lampert
Poet, Philosopher, and Educator

RED FLAGS OF DOOM AND GLOOM

Pay attention to the RED FLAGS of doom and gloom and heed their warnings. Everything in life has an expiration date.

Red Flag: Your teacher's assignments are insane. For example: Write a paper that covers the 12-18th century and examine the political, religious, cultural, and social changes that occurred. In this case, it is best to write an anonymous letter to the dean and the teacher, attach the ridiculous assignment, and let the dean and teacher work it out on their own.

Red Flag: Your partner is no longer interested in you. For example: Your partner no longer uses the pronoun "we" with regard to planning for the future. It is time to let go of this relationship and find a new love.

Red Flag: Your employer is having a business setback and will have to fire some employees to stay afloat. It is time to start looking for a new part-time job.

Let's Recap: Manage Your Anxiety, Stress and Depression
Here is the list of seven stresses that are mentioned in this chapter. The first six stresses can be managed, solved, and resolved with the tools and techniques contained within this book. The seventh stress cannot be made **RIGHT** because life is **UNFAIR.** The best policy is to pay attention to the **RED FLAGS OF DOOM AND GLOOM** and change course to safer ground.

1. Time Management Tools (Chapter 1 and 2)
- Smartgrades Academic Planner (fully loaded)
- To Do List: Big Picture and Many Details
- Set Priorities: Urgent, Important, Low, Optional
- Divide and Conquer: Breakdown Big Tasks
- Use Time Logs: Estimate and Actual Time
- Prepare for Delays, Detours, and Distractions
- Manage Ten Different Types of Schedules

2. Organization: 6 Sets of Academic Facts (Chapter 2)
You will have to manage 3 sets of facts: Class notes, handouts, and textbook and 3 sets of Test Review Notes for each class.

3. Eat Right for Energy to Learn (Chapter 3)
- High Fiber Breakfast
- Power Lunch (big plate)
- Lite Dinner (small plate)
- Power Study Snacks

4. Daily Study Routine (Chapter 7)

- Eat right, sleep well, and exercise for energy to learn
- Right after class, write your Test-Review Notes
- Use your **SMARTGRADES SUCCESS STRATEGY** to process the facts for Instant & Total Recall to ace your exams
- Study Periods: 45 Minute study periods with 15 Minute study breaks (stretch, Power Study Snack, and drink)

5. Financial Stability (Chapter 14 and 15)

- Networking and First Business Card
- Summer Internships and First Job
- Resume and First Interview

6. Entrepreneurial Tools to Start Your Own Business

Minor in business and graduate with basic business skills, so that so will be able to start your own buisness.

7. Manage Worry, Anxiety, and Stress That Can Escalate into Depression and Suicide

- Pay attention to the **RED FLAGS**, the warning signs.
- Disappointments cause pain, rage, and depression.
- **LIFE IS UNFAIR.** Everything in life has an expiration date.
- Do not take prescription pills with dangerous side effects that prop you up and mask your painful feelings.
- **FEEL TO HEAL.** Grieve your losses. Let the tears roll down your face for days, weeks, or even years.
- Change course to safer ground

APRIL 30
Poetry In Your Pocket Day

BE BORN

Be Born.
Become Educated.
Love Your Work.
Make a Meaningful Contribution -
To Yourself, Your Family, and Humanity.
Be a True Friend to Yourself First.
Have Sex with Someone You Love.
Make Love with Complete Abandon.
Enjoy Unconditional Love from Your Devoted Pet.
Make Time to Read the Funnies and Laugh.
Save Enough Money to Visit the Popular,
Pretty, and Peaceful Places of the World.
Read Great Literature, Listen to Great Music,
See Great Art, Watch the Great Movies,
Play the Fun Sports, Dance till Dawn,
Taste the Great Culinary Delights of the World -
Eat Slowly, Enjoy Every Bite, and Stay in Shape.
Plan One Great Adventure and Stick to the Plan.
Grow Old and Wise. Leave Your Money to
Someone You Love - Who Loves You Back.
Die in Your Sleep.

Sharon Esther Lampert

www.WorldFamousPoems.com
The Greatest Poems Ever Written on Extraordinary World Events

The Sole Intention of My Poetry Is to Add LIGHT to Your Soul

THE 22 COMMANDMENTS
ALL YOU WILL EVER NEED TO KNOW ABOUT GOD
A UNIVERSAL MORAL COMPASS FOR ALL PEOPLE,
FOR ALL RELIGIONS, AND FOR ALL TIME

1. LIFE Over Death
2. STRENGTH Over Weakness
3. DEED Over Sin
4. LOVE Over Hatred
5. TRUTH Over Lie
6. WISDOM Over Stupidity
7. OPTIMISM Over Pessimism
8. SHARING Over Selfishness
9. PRAISE Over Criticism
10. LOYALTY Over Abandonment
11. RESPONSIBILITY Over Blame
12. GRATITUDE Over Envy
13. REWARD Over Punishment
14. ALLIES Over Enemies
15. CREATION Over Destruction
16. EDUCATION Over Ignorance
17. COOPERATION Over Competition
18. FREEDOM Over Oppression
19. COMPASSION Over Indifference
20. FORGIVENESS Over Revenge
21. PEACE Over War
22. JOY Over Suffering

Sharon Esther Lampert
Kadimah: 8th Prophetess of Israel

www.PoetryJewels.com
Diamonds, Emeralds, Sapphires, Rubies, and Pearls

The Sole Intention of My Poetry Is to Add LIGHT to Your Soul

PHOTON'S
Spiritual Illuminations

5 SUPER POWERS
TO MAKE YOUR DREAMS COME TRUE

1. TIME Is Nonrefundable
(Don't Waste Your Time)

2. ENERGY Is Rechargeable
(Set a Regular Bedtime)

3. MONEY Goes Round and Round
(You Have to Be in the Loop)

4. SELF-WORTH Is Infinite Potential
(Know Your Strengths, Iron Out Your weaknesses)

5. LOVE Everything You Touch
(Put Your Heart into Everything)

WORLD PEACE IS COMING TO PLANET EARTH
www.BooksNotBombs.com

PHOTON'S
Spiritual Illuminations

My Empowerment Affirmation

I have only one life.
My life is a valuable gift.
I am responsible for my destiny.
I changed my life to ensure my happiness.
Each day is lived fully with
purpose, enthusiasm, and joy.

He Who Asks a Question is a
Fool for Five Minutes;
He Who Does Not Ask a Question
Remains a Fool Forever!

Chinese Proverb

Chapter 6
Get the Most Out of Class

Try to Learn Something
About Everything
and Everything
About Something

Thomas Henry Huxley

Chapter 6
Get the Most Out of Class

Tools of the Trade

- Choose the Right School

- Choose the Right Classes

- Pick the Best Teachers

- Find the Best Supplementary Textbook to Learn

- How to Preread the Textbook Chapter Before Class

- How to Pack a Well Equipped Book Bag

- How to Use Active Listening Tools

- How to Use Abbreviated Note Taking Tools

- Classroom Do's and Don'ts

- Your Teacher's Office Hours

- Emergency Student Contact Information

- Visit the School's Tutoring Center

- Nine Good Reasons to Visit Your Teacher

How to Choose the Right School, Great Teachers, Practical Classes, and Best Learning Textbooks

Choose the Right School
Q1. Are you in the right school to pursue your goals for
the future?

Choose Practical Classes
Q2. Does the course have a practical application for your
future?

EVERY DAY AN EASY A

Choose Great Teachers

Q3. Did you pick the best teacher for the subject material?

Checkout the Course Syllabus
Before taking a class, make an appointment to visit the
teacher, and ask for a copy of the course syllabus to get
a general overview of the class requirements:

Q1. Do you have to take tests or write papers?

Q2. Are the tests multiple choice or essays?

Q3. How many research papers are required?

Q4. How many pages is a research paper assignment?

Q5. What are the recommended reading materials?

Q6. Is assigned textbook up-to-date?

Q7. Do class assignments have realistic time allotments?

Q8. Does teacher give out well-organized handouts?

Q9. Does teacher makes time to answer student questions?

Q10. Does teacher give fair tests?

DAILY ACTION PLAN

☐ Step 1. Visit teacher during office hours

☐ Step 2. Ask for a copy of the course syllabus

☐ Step 3. Speak to students who have taken the course

Make a list of the best teachers, classes, and extra-curricular activities in school

The highly recommended teachers in school are:

1.

2.

3.

4.

5.

The highly recommended practical classes in school are:

1.

2.

3.

4.

5.

The best places (no external distractions) to study are:

1.

2.

3.

4.

5.

The best extra-curricular activities in school are:

1.

2.

3.

4.

5.

Your Supplementary Textbooks

Quite often, the assigned textbook may not be the best learning tool, and you will have to go to the bookstore and find another textbook with better illustrations that makes it easier to understand the academic material.

Q. Did you find the best supplementary textbook to help you learn the course material?

The Day Before Class

Q. Did you preread the chapter before coming to class for maximum absorption of the academic material?

2 Hours Before Class

Q1. Do you have an alarm clock to wake you up early?

Q2. Did you take a 20-minute jog before class?

Q3. Did you eat a nutritious meal for the energy to learn?

Q4. Do you wear a watch to keep you on time?

Q5. Did you write a "Daily Action Plan"?

How to Pack a Well Equipped Book Bag

Q. Does your book bag contain the following supplies?

☐ 1. Smartgrades Academic Planner to keep track of your ten schedules and school assignments

☐ 2. Smartgrades School Notebook with 1000 learning tools at your fingertips

☐ 3. Pencil case filled with extra pens and pencils

☐ 4. Tissues for colds or for changing temperatures
(cold to hot or hot to cold) that will give you a
running nose.

☐ 5. NIVEA Lip baum for dry lips (baby blue cover is great)

☐ 6. Power Study Snacks for Energy to Learn

a. Trail mix and water bottle to stay hydrated

b. Oatmeal cookie, bran muffin

c. Apple, apricots, or dates

d. Turkey sandwich on whole grain bread, slice of tomato

☐ 7. Tape Recorder to Capture Lecture Notes

There are days when you will go to class and feel tired.
You didn't sleep well or eat right and have low energy.
Or you have a cold and don't feel well. This is the time
to use a tape recorder to make sure you get all the facts.

1. Tape recorder, blank tape, AA or AAA batteries.

2. Right after class, go back to bed and take a nap.

In Class: How to Choose the Right Seat

Q1. Are you sitting in a desk where you can clearly see
the blackboard and hear your teacher's lecture?

Q2. Are you sitting next to friends who talk during a lecture?

Q3. Are you sitting too close to the noisy air conditioner,
hallway, door (opens and closes), or window (street noise)?

Your Teacher's Office Hours *

Q. Do you have your teacher's office hours and phone
   number?

Class:

Teacher's Name:

Office Address:

Teacher's Office Hours:

Teacher's Office Phone Number:

Teacher's E-mail Address:

The Phone Number of a Study Buddy *

Do you have an emergency phone number of a student

in each of your classes in case you don't feel well and can't

come to class?

Class:

Student's Name:

Student's Phone Number:

Student's E-mail Address:

* A SMARTGRADES School Notebook contains a built-in

directory to record this information, and has 1000

learning tools at your fingertips.

Asking Questions in Class

Ask your teacher what he/she prefers. Should you raise your hand during a lecture, ask your questions at the end of the lecture, or go to the office after class and ask your question. Whatever the case, write down the questions so you don't forget them.

Example:

Q. "With all due respect, Professor, I am confused
   and in need of clarification of ....?"

My School's Tutoring Center

If you are having difficulty understanding a lesson,
go directly to the tutoring center for academic help.
Visit Tutoring Center:

Q1. What is the phone number of the tutoring center?

Q2. What is the director's name?

Q3. Where is the tutoring center located?

Q4. When is it open?

Q5. Do you have to make an appointment or can you
     walk-in?

My Private Learning Specialist

If you can afford private tutoring sessions, set up your sessions as soon as possible because your tutor may not be available when you are in need of assistance.

Steps to Success

Step 1. Preread Your Textbook Chapter Before Class

If you preread the textbook chapter before class, all of the academic material will be familiar, and you will have a higher level of absorption and greater understanding.

Step 2. Practice Active Listening During Class

According to research studies, we remember a dismal 25-50% of what we hear. Listening is therefore a skill that we can all benefit from improving. The way to become a better listener is to practice "active listening" as follows:

- ☑ Sit at a desk where you can clearly see and hear the teacher.

- ☑ Look at the teacher directly, nod, and smile.

- ☑ Clear your mind of all internal distractions.

- ☑ If internal thoughts interfere, write them down and deal with them later. If you are hungry, you will not be able to ignore your hunger pain, so make sure you eat something with fiber (no cravings) before class, e.g., bran muffin.

- ☑ Ignore all external distractions, e.g., cellphone.

- ☑ Stop forming counter arguments while the other person is speaking.

Step 3. Use Active Note-Taking Skills During Class
When you take notes, restate a message with fewer words, and locate the main point.

Topic:
Main Ideas:
Supporting Examples, Evidence, Explanations:

Step 4. Use Abbreviations to Take Quick Notes

For example = e.g.

Step 5. Use a Tape Recorder to Record the Lecture
A tape recorder allows you to spend more time listening and learning and less time stressing out over note taking.

Step 6. Ask Questions in Class

Seek clarification by asking a question:

Q. "What do you mean when you say..."

Step 7. Ask Questions About Test
When the teacher gives you a date for the test, ask questions about the test, such as:
Q1. What is the format of the test?
Q2. How many questions are on the test?
Q3. What topics are covered? What is not covered?
Q4. How does the test count toward percentage of grade?
Q5. How is test scored? Is there a penalty for guessing?
Q6. Are there sample exams on file in the library?
Q7. Is the test cumulative?

Step 8. Write Down the Homework Assignment
Don't memorize the homework assignment, write it down in your **SMARTGRADES** Homework Action Planner, and check it twice for accuracy.

How to Preread a Textbook Chapter

Before class, preread the textbook chapter to increase your understanding and absorption of the academic material.

Step 1. Read the End-of-Chapter Summary

Read the end-of-chapter summary for an overview of the main points of the chapter.

Step 2. Read the Boldface Headings of the Chapter

Read for a general overview of the material of the chapter. Read the boldface headings and subheadings. Read actively with a pencil/highlighter in hand and write down the main idea and major and minor points of the chapter.

Main Idea:

Major Points:
1.
2.
3.

Minor Points:
1.
2.
3.

After Class Read Textbook for In-Depth Comprehension

After class, you will go back to your class notes, handouts, and textbook and read for in-depth comprehension and write Test Review Notes. You will use your, **SMARTGRADES SUCCESS STRATEGY** to process academic material for Instant & Total Recall to ace your exams (Chapter 7).

Your Teacher's Office Hours

Here are nine very good reasons to visit your teacher:

☑ **Visit 1: Introduction**
Visit your teacher to introduce yourself.

☑ **Visit 2: Seek Clarification**
Visit your teacher to ask a question.

☑ **Visit 3: Approval of Topic and Outline of Paper**
Visit your teacher for approval of topic and outline of your paper.

☑ **Visit 4: Approval of Rough Draft of Paper**
Visit your teacher for approval of rough draft of your paper.

☑ **Visit 5: Teacher's Comments**
Visit your teacher to discuss comments on your paper.

☑ **Visit 6: Unfair Test Question**
Visit your teacher to complain about an unfair test question.

☑ **Visit 7: Grading Error**
Visit your teacher to complain about a grading error.

☑ **Visit 8: Express Gratitude**
Visit your teacher to say thank you to express your appreciation for a great class.

☑ **Visit 9: Recommendation for Your Resume**
Visit your teacher to ask for a recommendation to accompany your resume.

Classroom Do's

1. Do come to class prepared, having completed the reading assignments.

2. Do come to class with energy to learn: Nutritious breakfast, sufficient sleep, and daily exercise.

3. Do show up on time for class.

4. Do sit in the front rows of the classroom.

5. Do come to class with proper school supplies: Pens, pencils, sharpener, eraser, textbook, Smartgrades School Notebook and Academic Planner.

6. Do develop a positive mental attitude about school and your goals.

7. Do your best to be sure that your work is done to your best ability, and within deadlines.

8. Do let the teacher know when you must miss class or an exam in advance, whenever possible.

9. Do ask questions in class when you do not understand the teacher's explanation.

Classroom Don'ts

1. Don't walk in or out of class while the class is in session to go to the bathroom or answer a cellphone.

2. Don't overparticipate in class discussions. Give others a chance to contribute to the discussion.

3. Don't call your teacher at home unless you have permission to do so.

4. Don't leave class early. This is disruptive and rude.

5. Don't correct the teacher in front of the class.

6. Don't have side conversations with students during class.

7. If you have a question, ask the teacher, not another student, or you will both be lost.

8. Don't act disinterested, pompous, or bored during class.

9. Every class is important. If you are absent from class, don't ask your teacher if you missed anything important.

10. If you have a problem it is best to see the teacher first. Don't go over the teacher's head unless you have to.

11. Don't sit in the last seat in the backrow of the classroom when there are empty seats available up front.

Let's Recap: How to Get the Most Out of Class

1. Preread Textbook Chapter
   Q. Did you preread the textbook chapter for maximum absorption of the academic material?

2. Eat Right for Energy to Learn
   Q. Did you eat a high fiber breakfast before class?

3. Choose the Right Seat
   Q. Did you choose a seat where you can see and hear?

4. Active Listening Skills
   Q. Did you learn how to focus your attention to avoid external and internal distractions?

5. Active Note Taking Skills
   Q. Did you locate the main ideas and supporting details?

6. Abbreviation Skills
   Q. Did you abbreviate repetitive words?

7. Asking Questions in Class
   Q. Did you ask a question to clarify confusion?

8. Asking Questions About the Test
   1. Did you ask about the kind of test?
   2. Are there sample exams filed in the library?
   3. How is the test scored?

9. Homework Assignment Skills
   Q. Did you write down the homework assignment in a Smartgrades Academic Planner (not in your head or on a piece of scrap paper)?

Q. Did you check the assignment twice for accuracy?

The More You Understand,
The Less You Have to Remember.

Craig A. McCraw

SMARTGRADES PROCESSING TOOLS

In 24 Hours, F Students Become A Students

Sharon Rose Sugar
The Paladin of Education for the 21st Century

THIS BOOK SAVES LIVES
"The Silent Crisis Destroying America's Brightest Minds"
"Book of the Month" Alma Public Library, Wisconsin

Chapter 7

SMARTGRADES
SUCCESS STRATEGY
ACE EVERY TEST EVERY TIME
Instant and Total Recall
Write Test Review Notes
Ace Test

SMARTGRADES SUCCESS STRATEGY
ACE EVERY TEST EVERY TIME

Step 1.   Estimation Tool
Step 2.   Divide and Conquer Tool
Step 3.   Active Reading Tool
Step 4.   Extraction Tool
Step 5.   Condensation Tool
Step 6.   Association Tool
Step 7.   Test Review Note Tool
Step 8.   Conversion Tool
Step 9.   Visualization Tool
Step 10. Self Test Tool

In-Depth Comprehension
Long Term Retention
Mastery of the Material

Chapter 7

SMARTGRADES
SUCCESS STRATEGY
ACE EVERY TEST EVERY TIME
Instant & Total Recall

Are You Test Ready?

Education is food for the brain. Students spend the entire day eating facts and building their brain muscles. If I give you a sandwich to eat, you cannot stuff the entire sandwich into your mouth. You have to take small bites and chew, chew, chew, and digest. Eating facts is like eating a sandwich. You have to take small amounts of information and chew (in-depth comprehension), chew (long term retention), and chew (mastery of academic material).

Right after every class, go directly to your study area and write your Test Review Notes to process (absorb) the facts for Instant & Total Recall to ace your exams.

DAILY ACTION PLAN
- ☑ 1. Get up early enough eat a fiber-fuel breakfast
- ☑ 2. Preread the textbook chapter for maximum absorption
- ☑ 3. Go to class to receive teacher's wisdom and experience
- ☑ 4. Go to a well equipped study room
- ☑ 5. Write Test Review Notes for class notes, handouts, and textbook
- ☑ 6. To ace a test use your **SMARTGRADES SUCCESS STRATEGY** for Instant & Total Recall of the facts

SMARTGRADES SUCCESS STRATEGY

To ace your exams, you have to develop three critical skills:

RETENTION, RECOGNITION, RECALL

1. **RETENTION** is your ability to absorb the facts.

2. **RECOGNITION** is reading the test question and knowing the answer.

3. **INSTANT RECALL** is popping out an answer in a jiffy.

4. **TOTAL RECALL** is long term retention of all of the facts.

To acquire these 3 skills, you need **REVIEW** and **REPETITION**.

Here Are the 5 R's of Test Preparation
REVIEW, REPETITION, RETENTION, RECOGNITION, RECALL

The academic facts have to be processed (absorption) for Instant & Total Recall to ace your test. You have to eat facts, just like you eat food. The facts have to be digested. **SMART-GRADES SUCCESS STRATEGY** is a 10 step learning tool for Instant & Total Recall of the facts. Let's define each of the following terms:

Step 1. Estimation Tool
Step 2. Divide and Conquer Tool
Step 3. Active Reading Tool
Step 4. Extraction Tool
Step 5. Condensation Tool
Step 6. Association Tool
Step 7. Test Review Note Tool
Step 8. Conversion Tool
Step 9. Visualization Tool
Step 10. Self-Test Tool

Step 1. Estimation Tool
Every paragraph contains one main idea and many supporting details. If you have ten paragraphs, then you have ten main ideas.

Step 2. Divide and Conquer Tool
You have to process one paragraph at a time for Instant & Total Recall. You cannot stuff a whole sandwich into your mouth. You have to take small bites, chew, chew, chew, and digest.

Step 3. Active Reading Tool
When you read, you need to be holding a pencil like a fisherman holds a net over the water to capture a fish. You are fishing for the facts. Every fact is a test question.

Step 4. Extraction Tool
You job is to extract the main idea and supporting details of every paragraph: Who, What, Where, When, and Why.

Step 5. Condensation Tool
Your job is to condense the facts and make them easier to digest, absorb, and process for Instant & Total Recall.

Step 6. Association Tool
Association links the unknown fact to a known fact in your mind. This is the glue that makes the facts stick to you.

Step 7. Test Review Note Tool
Your class notes, handouts, and textbook have to be processed for Instant & Total Recall to ace your tests.

Step 8. Conversion Tool
The facts have to be converted into test questions.

Step 9. Visualization Tool
Q. What type of test question is best suited for the facts?

Step 10. Self-Testing Tool
You have to answer your test questions to make sure that you have Instant & Total Recall and can ace your tests.

How to Process (Absorb) the Facts to Ace a Test

Tools of the Trade

SMARTGRADES SUCCESS STRATEGY
ACE EVERY TEST EVERY TIME

Steps to Success

Step 1. Gather Study Materials and Go to Study Area
- ☐ a. Class Notes
- ☐ b. Handouts
- ☐ c. Textbook

Step 2. Choose a Great Study Area
- ☐ a. No external distractions
- ☐ b. Good lighting
- ☐ c. Comfortable chair
- ☐ d. Big desk to hold all school supplies

Step 3. Clear Your Mind of Internal Negative Distractions
a. Worry and Anxiety: "I feel overwhelmed by workload!"
b. Fear of Failure: "I feel inadequate...I can't keep up!"
c. Negative Self-Talk: "I am not smart enough!"

Step 4. Develop Positive Self-Talk to Build Your Self-Esteem
a. "I have the power to make my dreams come true!"
b. "I have the power to transform weakness into strength!"
c. "I have the power to change bad habits into good habits!"
d. "I have the power to focus my mind on the task at hand!"

Step 5. Develop a Regular Study Period Schedule

Q1. Where do I study best:

☐ At Home   ☐ In the Library   ☐ Somewhere Else

Q2. When do I study best:

☐ In the Morning   ☐ Afternoon   ☐ Evening

Q3. How do I study best:

☐ Alone   ☐ With a Friend   ☐ In a Group

Q4. I need to take a break:

☐ Every 30 Minutes   ☐ Every Hour   ☐ Every Two Hours

Example: Weekly Study Period Schedule

M: Study: 2-7 p.m.

T: Study: 2-7 p.m.

W: Study: 2-7 p.m.

T: Study: 2-7 p.m.

F: No Classes   Study: 10-3 p.m.

S: Study: 12-3 p.m.

S: Study: 1-4 p.m.

Step 6. Plan Regular Study Periods Plan with Study Breaks

Study for 50 minutes and then take a 10 minute study break:

2-2:50   10 minute break   Write Class Notes Test Review Notes

3-3:50   10 minute break   Write Textbook Test Review Notes

4-4:50   10 minute break   Write Handout Test Review Notes

5-5:50   10 minute break   Write Rough Draft of Paper

6-6:50   10 minute break   Do Math Homework

Step 7. Right After Class, Write Your Test Review Notes

SMARTGRADES SUCCESS STRATEGY

1. Estimation Tool
How Many Main Ideas?
Every paragraph contains one main idea and many supporting details. If you have ten paragraphs, then you have ten main ideas.

Example: Estimate Main Ideas
1 main idea per paragraph
10 paragraphs = 10 main ideas

Paragraph 1
Main Idea:

Paragraph 2
Main Idea:

Paragraph 3
Main Idea:

---

2. Divide and Conquer Tool
You have to process one paragraph at a time for Instant & Total Recall. You cannot stuff a whole sandwich into your mouth. You have to take small bites, chew, chew, chew, and digest.

Paragraph 1
Main Idea:
Supporting Details:
Condense Facts:
Association Cue for Instant & Total Recall:
Possible Test Question:

3. Active Reading Tool

When you read, you need to be holding a pencil like a fisherman holds a net over the water to capture a fish. You are fishing for the facts. Every fact is a test question. Underline the <u>main idea</u> and <u>supporting details.</u>

Example: Underline Main Idea and Supporting Details
<u>Thomas Jefferson</u> was an intellectual, statesman, and <u>third president of the United States.</u> Although Jefferson served as <u>governor of Virginia, ambassador to France, secretary of state, vice president, and president,</u> he is remembered in history less for the offices he held than for what he stood for.

---

4. Extraction Tool

You job is to extract the main idea and supporting details of every paragraph: Who, What, Where, When, and Why.

Example: Extract Facts
<u>Thomas Jefferson</u> was an intellectual, statesman, and <u>third president of the United States.</u> Although Jefferson served as <u>governor of Virginia, ambassador to France, secretary of state, vice president, and president,</u> he is remembered in history less for the offices he held than for what he stood for.

One Main Idea   Many Supporting Details

Main Idea: Thomas Jefferson, 3rd President of U.S.A.

Many Supporting Details:
- Held many offices
- President
- Vice President
- Ambassador
- Secretary of State

5. Condensation Tool

Your job is to condense the facts and make them easier to digest, absorb, and process for Instant & Total Recall.

Many Supporting Details:
- Held many offices
- President
- Vice President
- Ambassador
- Secretary of State

Example:Condense Facts
Held Many Offices = P/VP/AM/SS

---

6. Association Tool for Instant & Total Recall

Association links the unknown fact to a known fact in your mind. Choose the Association Cue that works best for you. Personal memory is the most powerful Association Cue.

Example: Associate Facts
P/VP/AM/SS = Association Cue = Personal Memory

My Personal Association Cue Is:
PVP played on AM radio on weekends (Sat, Sun)
Totally ridiculous memory cue, but it works for me

---

7. Test Review Note Tool

Your class notes, handouts, and textbook have to be processed for Instant & Total Recall to ace your tests.

☐ a. Test Review Note for Class Notes

☐ b. Test Review Note for Handouts

☐ c. Test Review Note for Textbook Chapter

My Test Review Note
Main Idea:
Supporting Details:
Condense Facts:
Association Cue for Instant & Total Recall:
Possible Test Question

---

8 & 9: Visualization and Conversion Tool

Visualize test question and convert facts, the main idea, and supporting details into a sample test question.

Q. What type of test question is best suited for the facts?

Sample Test Question

Q.   What positions did Thomas Jefferson hold?
(a)   3rd President of U.S.A.
(b)   Governor of Virginia
(c)   Ambassador to France
(d)   Secretary of State U.S.A.
(e)   Vice President of U.S.A.
(g)   All of the Above

---

10. Self-Testing Tool for Instant & Total Recall

To ace a test, you need to process (absorb) the facts for long-term retention. Cramming facts for short-term retention does not work because you won't have Instant & Total Recall of the facts and you will not ACE your test.

Q1. Can you recall the facts in a jiffy for Instant Recall?
Q2. Can you recall all of the facts for Total Recall?

If you can't remember the fact, change the association cue.

My Test Review Notes:
Time Log
Estimate: 5 Hours
Actual:
Error:
Speedbumps: Delays, Detours, or Distractions?

How to Associate Facts for Instant & Total Recall

The facts have to be processed for Instant & Total Recall to ace your test. To process the facts for long-term retention, you have to link the **UNKNOWN** fact to a **KNOWN** fact in your mind. This linking process is called Association.
For example, here are two unknown words:

Yin   Yan**g**

One of these words is male and the other word is female. The word Yang is male. To process the fact for Instant & Total Recall, we want to associate the fact, that is link the **unknown** fact to a **known** fact in our mind.

Association

Unknown Fact	LINK	**Known** Fact in Mind
Yan**g** (male)	LINK	"g looks like a penis"

The letter "g' on the Yang looks like a male penis. You will remember this fact in an Instant and you will remember this for a lifetime. We linked the **unknown** fact to a **known** fact in your mind. This is how to achieve **Instant & Total Recall** of the facts.

Steps to Success

Step 1. Selection
Select facts to memorize: Main ideas and Supporting Details (who, what, where, when why, and how).

Step 2. Association

Choose the association cue that fits your learning style.

Acronym Cue: Use letters to condense the key facts. For example, to remember how to shoot a rifle, use the classic acronym BRASS, which stands for: Breath, Relax, Aim, Sight, Squeeze.

Acrostic Cue: Use a sentence to condense the key facts. For example, to remember the order of G-clef notes on sheet music, (E, G, B, D, F) use the classic acrostic: Every Good Boy Deserves Fun.

Rhyme Cue: Use rhymes to link the key facts together. For example, the classic,"I before E, except after C."

Music Cue: Make up a song or poem with the information in it. Sing the song or recite the poem several times.

Chaining Cue: Create a story where each word or idea you have to remember cues the next idea you need to recall. Use your imagination. If you had to remember the name, Shirley Temple, you could rhyme Shirley with curly and remember that she had curly hair around her temples.

Funny Cue: Write a joke that contains the key facts. The funniest, most outlandish, and the strangest concoction of memory cues makes memorizing easy.

EVERY DAY AN EASY A

SMARTGRADES PROCESSING TOOLS

My Test Review Notes to Ace the Test

Paragraph 1
• Extract Facts:
Main Idea:
Supporting Details:
a.
b.
c.

• Condense Facts:

• Associate Facts:

• Convert to Test Question:
Q. Who, What, Where, When, Why, How?

• Self-Test for Instant and Total Recall

Paragraph 2
• Extract Facts:
Main Idea:
Supporting Details:
a.
b.
c.

• Condense Facts:

• Associate Facts:

• Convert to Test Question:
Q. Who, What, Where, When, Why, How?

• Self-Test for Instant and Total Recall

Paragraph 3

• Extract Facts:
Main Idea:
Supporting Details:
a.
b.
c.
• Condense Facts:

• Associate Facts:

• Convert to Test Question:
Q. Who, What, Where, When, Why, How?

• Self-Test for Instant and Total Recall

Paragraph 4

• Extract Facts:
Main Idea:
Supporting Details:
a.
b.
c.

• Condense Facts:

• Associate Facts:

• Convert to Test Question:
Q. Who, What, Where, When, Why, How?

• Self-Test for Instant and Total Recall

How to Develop a Study Group

Study groups can keep you and your friends on track for academic success. These groups help everyone because they facilitate the learning process by thinking out loud, sharing ideas, and learning from each other.

There are many benefits to forming a study group:

1. Improves your understanding of the material

2. Share your talents

3. Provides an emotional support system to motivate you

4. Learning can be drudgery and sharing the tedious task lessens the pain.

Tools of the Trade

How many students?
Who should be in the study group?
Where should you hold the study sessions?
How long should a study session be?
When should the study group meet?
Who is the leader of the group?
What are the objectives and goals?

Steps to Success

Step 1. How Many Students?

The best size for a study group is four to six people. Small groups don't have man power to get things done. Large groups are harder to manage.

Step 2. Who Are the Members?

The best study groups are composed of individuals who share the same interest in doing well in class and on tests. Everyone has different strengths and weakness. By participating in a study group you are able to benefit from the talents of other group members.

Step 3: Where Do We Meet?

Study group sessions should be held in a location where you can talk and bring your power study snacks. The best place is an empty classroom, office space or dining room table.

Step 4. How Long Do We Study?

Study group sessions should be not longer than two to three hours. If the study session is too short, you can't accomplish anything. If it is too long, you loose interest and focus. Its best to schedule breaks every 45 minutes for a ten minute study snack.

Step 5. When Do We Meet?

Try to meet at the same time and place each week. Creating a set routine will help each member to plan ahead and come prepare to each session.

Step 6. Who Is the Leader of the Group?

Each group study session should have a leader. It's the leaders responsibility to make sure that the group is focused and stays on track.

Step 7. What Are the Objectives of the Study Group?

Doing well in school is all about retrieving the facts from your class notes, handouts and textbook reading assignments, and then returning the facts on a test. The facts have to processed (absorbed) for Instant & Total Recall to ace your tests.

Each member can contribute their own particular strength to the group. Instead of one student doing all of the study tasks, they can be divided up among the study group. It is best to make a list of the tasks and divide and conquer, as follows:

Example: Divide Up Academic Tasks Among Members

1. One member takes copious notes in class.

2. One member collates the best supplementary reading materials to further a deeper understanding of the material.

3. One member has a good reparte with the teacher, visits the office once a week, and has a crystal clear understanding of the teacher's expectations.

4. One member collates old exams for practice test questions.

5. One member prepares power study snacks.

6. Three members divide up writing Test Review Notes
    a. Class Notes Test Review Notes
    b. Handouts Test Review Notes
    c. Textbook Test Review Notes

7. One member prereads the chapter, takes notes, and hands them out an hour before class.

What Is Your Learning Style

How to Understand Your Learning Style

Identifying and understanding your learning style is critical to your study preparation. By knowing how you learn best you can select a school, class, teacher, textbook, and ultimately a career that appeals to your unique way of learning things.

Tools of the Trade

Visual (most common)
Auditory (languages, music)
Tactile (kinesthetic)
Logical (mathematical)
Social (interpersonal)

Steps to Success

Read definitions below to figure out how you learn best.

Visual Learning Style
Students learn best when ideas or subjects are presented in a visual format, with pictures, diagrams, videos or overhead projectors.

Auditory Learning Style

Students are able to learn, understand and retain information better when they hear it rather than see it. Students learn by participating in class discussion, by listening to a teacher lecture, or listening to audio tapes. For example, students who excel at learning languages and composing music are auditory learners.

Tactile Learning Style

Tactile learners are hands-on learners. They learn by touching and feeling. They learn best when they are able to physically participate directly in what they are required to learn or understand. For example, students who excel at work which requires hands-on skills, such as dentistry, surgery or carpentry.

Solitary Learning Style

Students who are private, introspective and independent. They are able to concentrate and focus on a specific project without outside help. Solitary learners prefer to work on problems in isolation. For example, writers, scientists, and entrepreneurs are solitary learners.

Logical Learning Style

Students who prefer to use their brain for logical and mathematical reasoning prefer the logical learning style. Logical learners can recognize patterns easily and are good at making logical connections between what would appear to most people to be meaningless content.

Social Learning Style

Students who communicate well will others, both verbally and non-verbally. Social learners prefer learning in groups or classes and typically like to spend one-on-one time with a teacher or an instructor. For example, teachers and therapists are good listeners and are able to understand other's views.

1. What is your learning style?

2. How does understanding your learning style help you to make informed choices about your destiny?

3. Do you now understand why you would rather go to your room and write a book or become a teacher and work with a group, rather than work with your hands and become a dentist, like your father?

4. What career choices fit your learning style best?

SMART POWER IS BACK IN THE HANDS OF ALL STUDENTS
"If you need my help, I am at your service."
PHOTON
SUPERHERO OF EDUCATION
Earn A Grade
Earn Free Gift!
WORLD PEACE IS COMING TO PLANET EARTH
www.booksnotbombs.com

PHOTON'S
INTRODUCTION TO WRITING

WORLD PREMIERE!
Writing Is an Art Form
10 Esoteric Laws of Genius and Creativity (Chapter 11)

1. V.E.S.S.E.L.
2. INSPIRATION
3. IMPREGNATION
4. INCUBATION
5. GENESIS
6. SILENT: LISTEN
7. METAPHORPHOSIS
8. REVELATION
9. SIGNATURE
10. IMMORTALITY

How to Write a Grade A Paper

- Research Topic (Chapter 8)
- Choose a Researchable Topic
- Find Experts in Field
- Use Direct and Indirect Quotes
- Read Primary Source Material
- List Pro and Con Arguments
- Paraphrase Facts (in your own words)
- Apply Critical Thinking Tools (Chapter 10)
- Outline Main Ideas and Supporting Details
- Writing is Rewriting: Rough Draft to Final Draft

Use Standard Paper Organization:
Introduction, Body, and Conclusion

Use Standard Paragraph Organization:
5 Sentences: Intro, Quote, Example, Analysis, Conclusion

Use Transition Words to Bridge Ideas:
According to, For example, As a result, In conclusion,

Add Citations: Footnotes or Endnotes
Add Bibliography

Proofread Paper to Perfection (Chapter 9)
Grammar, Spelling, Punctuation, Neatness

There's No Such Thing
As Good Writing.
There's Only Good Rewriting.

Mark Twain

Chapter 8, Part I
Read, Write, and Proofread

English Essays
Research Papers

English is a unique language. Why is the word phonetic not spelled the way it sounds? There's no egg in eggplant, no ham in hamburger, neither apple nor pine in pineapple. English muffins weren't invented in England nor French fries in France. Quicksand can work slowly, boxing rings are square, and a guinea pig is neither from Guinea, nor is it a pig. The plural of tooth is teeth, so why isn't the plural of booth beeth? If you wrote a letter, perhaps you bote your tongue? People recite at a play, and play at a recital; ship by truck, and send cargo by ship; have noses that run, and feet that smell; park on driveways, and drive on parkways. A slim chance and a fat chance mean the same, but a wise man and a wise guy are opposites. Overlook and oversee are opposites, while quite a lot and quite a few are alike. A house can burn up as it burns down, a form can be filled in by being filled out, an alarm clock goes off by going on. On the other hand, so to speak, some things are talked about only when they are absent; i.e., we do not hear about a horseful carriage or a strapful gown, a sung hero or required love, someone who is combobulated, gruntled, ruly, or peccable.

Unknown Internet Quote

Chapter 8
Write an A Grade Paper

Tools of the Trade

Research Topic
Choose Researchable Topic
Use Library Databases
Use Encyclopedia for General Overview
Find Experts in Field
Read Primary Sources (autobiographical)
Read Secondary Sources (biographical)
List Pro and Con Arguments
Paraphrase Research (in your own words)
Use Direct and Indirect Quotes
Document Source Material: MLA, APA, Chicago Style

Write Paper
Write Outline
Write Thesis Statement
Use Standard Paper Structure
Use Standard Paragraph Structure
Use Transition Words to Bridge Paragraphs and Ideas
Apply Critical Thinking Tools (Chapter 10)
Seek Teacher's Approval for Outline and Rough Drat
Write Final Draft
Add Citations: Footnotes or Endnotes
Add Bibliography
Proofread Paper to Perfection (Chapter 9)

There Are Four Basic Types of Essays:
Description, Narration, Exposition, Persuasion

Each of these types of essays has its distinctive characteristics; however, you will find that essays are often a combination of the various forms.

1. Expository

2. Descriptive

3. Explanatory

4. Illustrative

5. Analytical

6. Argumentative

7. Defining

8. Evaluative

9. Interpretive

Definitions of Essays

1. **Expository:** An essay to convey "information."

2. **Descriptive:** An essay that describes something or someone, a situation or a location.

3. **Explanatory:** An essay that looks for reasons or causes in relation to perceived effects or results based on theory.

4. **Illustrative:** An essay that is fairly descriptive, but illustrations need to be relevant and appropriate, and written with explicit reference to the theoretical point being supported.

5. **Analytical:** An essay for experimental data. It is the process of breaking down something into its component parts, often in order to analyse patterns or categories based on a theoretical position.

6. **Argumentative:** An essay of debate and disagreement.

7. **Defining:** An essay based on a definition of terms.

8. **Evaluative:** An essay that requires you to pass judgement or make an assessment, according to stated criteria.

9. **Interpretive:** An essay where your interpretation is examined in the context of other more established interpretations.

A Simple Overview of Essay Paper

Steps to Success

Step 1. Restatement of Essay Question

Read essay question and restate question as the topic sentence of essay.

Here is a sample essay question:

Q. If your doctor told you that you had only a few months to live, how would you alter your way of life? Discuss.

To answer this essay question, first restate the question as the introductory sentence of your essay, as follows:

If (my) doctor told (me) that (I) had only a few months to live, (I) would alter (my) way of life by... add on the facts.

Step 2. Write Outline of Essay to Organize Thoughts

Write outline of main ideas and supporting examples.

Essay Outline

Main Idea 1. Spend more time with loved ones

Supporting Example: Take pictures for a lasting legacy

Main Idea 2. Visit the beautiful places on earth

Supporting Example: Take a trip to Hawaii

Step 3. Use Standard Essay and Paragraph Structure

Use standard essay structure: Introduction, Body, and Conclusion.

Introduction	Introduce Topic Introduce Main Ideas 1, 2, and 3
Body	Paragraph 1 Introduce Main Idea 1 Add: Supporting Example Add: Direct or Indirect Quote Add: Analysis, Critical Thinking Tools Add: Concluding Sentence Add: Transition Words to Link Ideas
Body	Paragraph 2 Introduce Main Idea 2 Add: Supporting Example Add: Direct or Indirect Quote Add: Analysis, Critical Thinking Tools Add: Concluding Sentence Add: Transition Words to Link Ideas
Body	Paragraph 3 Introduce Main Idea 3 Add: Supporting Example Add: Direct or Indirect Quote Add: Analysis, Critical Thinking Tools Add: Concluding Sentence Add: Transition Words to Link Ideas
Conclusion	Restate Introduction and Main Ideas Final Thoughts

Research Topic

Tools of the Trade

How to Use Library Databases
Use Encyclopedia for General Overview of Topic
List Experts in Field
List Pro and Con Arguments
Read Primary Sources (Autobiographical)
Read Secondary Sources (Biographical)
Document Sources: MLA, APA, Chicago Style
Paraphrase Don't Plagiarize
Organize: Smartgrades Research School Notebook
Take Control of Your Time with Time Logs

Steps to Success

Step 1. Use Encyclopedia for General Overview of Topic
Q. Who are the experts in the field?
    1st Expert:

    2nd Expert:

    3rd Expert:

Step 2. Read Bibliographic Notes for a List of Primary and Secondary Source Materials on the Topic

Q. How many source materials are required for paper?

1. Primary Source (autobiographical):
    Book:
    Author:
    Publisher:
    Copyright:
    Page #

2. Primary Source (autobiographical):
Book:
Author:
Publisher:
Copyright:
Page #

3. Secondary Source (biographical):
Book:
Author:
Publisher:
Copyright:
Page #

Step 3. Read Primary and Secondary Source Materials for Pro and Con Arguments and Quotes (Direct and Indirect).

Expert in Field:
Pro Argument:
Direct or Indirect Quote:
Citation: Book, Author, Publisher, Copyright, Page #

Expert in Field:
Pro Argument:
Direct or Indirect Quote:
Citation: Book, Author, Publisher, Copyright, Page #

Expert in Field:
Con Argument:
Direct or Indirect Quote:
Citation: Book, Author, Publisher, Copyright, Page #

Research Topic
Time Log
Estimate Time: 10 Hours
Actual Time:
Error:
Speedbumps: Any Delays, Detours, and Distractions?

Use Library Databases

Libraries are divided into reading rooms, restricted collections, and unrestricted book stacks.

Unrestricted Book Stacks:

• Anyone can use and read in the library, or take home

Restricted Collections:

• Special collections of rare books

• Open to Scholars, or to those with credentials

Libraries contain circulating and non-circulating materials for use only in the library, e.g., reference materials.

Step 1. Use Encyclopedia for General Overview of Topic
The leading encyclopedias are:
• Britannica
• Americana
• Collier's
• World Book

Step 2. Use Card Catalog for Primary and Secondary Sources
This is a list of all of the books in the library. The books are indexed by subject, author, and title.

Step 3. Use Newspaper Indexes for Most Recent News
Many large city newspapers provide an indexed list of all published articles.

Step 4. Use Periodical Indexes for Most Recent News
The most popular magazine articles are published in
"The Readers' Guide to Periodical Literature."

Step 5. Use the Vertical File
This file contains pamphlets and brochures.

Step 6. Use the U.S. Documents Monthly Catalog
This is useful for locating government publications.

How is Your Library Organized

Most libraries use the Dewey Decimal Classification System.
This system uses numbers 000-999 to classify all materials
by subject matter.

The Dewey Classification System

000 - 099	General
100 - 199	Philosophy
200 - 299	Religion
300 - 399	Social Sciences
400 - 499	Language
500 - 599	Science
600 - 699	Useful Arts
700 - 799	Fine Arts
800 - 899	Literature
900 -999	History

Library of Congress Classification System
This system uses letters to denote major categories.

A GENERAL WORKS
B PHILOSOPHY. PSYCHOLOGY. RELIGION
C AUXILIARY SCIENCES OF HISTORY
D WORLD HISTORY AND HISTORY OF EUROPE, ASIA, AFRICA, AUSTRALIA, NEW ZEALAND, ETC.
E HISTORY OF THE AMERICAS
F HISTORY OF THE AMERICAS
G GEOGRAPHY. ANTHROPOLOGY. RECREATION
H SOCIAL SCIENCES
J POLITICAL SCIENCE
L EDUCATION
M MUSIC AND BOOKS ON MUSIC
N FINE ARTS
P LANGUAGE AND LITERATURE
Q SCIENCE
R MEDICINE
S AGRICULTURE
T TECHNOLOGY
U MILITARY SCIENCE
V NAVAL SCIENCE
Z BIBLIOGRAPHY. LIBRARY SCIENCE. INFORMATION RESOURCES (GENERAL)

Library Research
Time Log
Estimate: 20 Hours (Find Books, Read Books, Take Notes)
Actual Time:
Error:

Speedbumps: Any Delays, Detours, and Distractions?

Write a Thesis Statement

Tools of the Trade
Arguable Topic, Question, Point of View, and Defense

What is a Thesis?

A thesis statement declares what you believe and what you intend to prove. An effective thesis has a definable, arguable claim. You must do a lot of background reading before you know enough about a subject to identify key or essential questions. You may not know how you stand on an issue until you have examined the evidence.

Steps to Success

Step 1. Select a Topic.

Example
Topic: Television sex and violence

Step 2. Ask an Interesting Question

Example
Q. What are the effects of television sex and violence on children?

Step 3. Write a Thesis Statement (Point of View)

Example: Thesis Statement
Sex and violence on television increases aggressive behavior in preschool children.

Step 4. Defend Your Thesis Statement
Choose evidence that supports your Thesis Statement

Paraphrase Ideas of Others
How to Write it in Your Own Words

A paraphrase is restating the ideas of others in your own words and keeping the meaning intact.

Tools of the Trade

Original Source Material
"Unique Terminology"
Main Idea and Supporting Details
Keep Meaning Intact
Add Citation: Book, Author, Publisher, Copyright, Page #

Steps to Success

Step 1. Read original passage for in-depth comprehension.

Step 2. Write down main idea and supporting ideas.

Step 3. If you used any "unique terminology" from the passage put a quote around it.

Step 4. Cite the source to credit it.

Step 5. Rewrite original passage in your own words.

Example

Original Text

Aristotle is a Greek philosopher, scientist, and educator who lived from 384 to 322 B.C. He is considered one of the greatest and most influential philosophers in Western culture. He was born in northern Greece on the Macedonian coast, in a small town called Stagira.

List Main Idea and Supporting Details:
Main Idea: Aristotle, Greek Philosopher, Scientist, Educator
Supporting Details:
(a) 384 to 322 B.C.
(b) Born: Greece, Macedonian coast, town of Stagira
     Citation: Encyclopedia

Paraphrase Text

One of the most admired and respected philosophers in Western culture was a man named Aristotle (384 to 322 B.C.). He was born in Greece in the small town of Stagira that is located on the Macedonian coast (citation: encyclopedia).

Paraphrase Source Material
Time Log
Estimate Time: 10 Hours
Actual Time:
Error:
Speedbumps: Any Delays, Detours, and Distractions?

Write Outline of Paper

Tools of the Trade

List Experts in Field
List Pro and Con Arguments
List Arguments from Most Important to Least Important
Add Citations: Book, Author, Publisher, Copyright, Page #
Organize: Smartgrades Research School Notebook
Take Control of Your Time with Time Logs
See Teacher for Approval of Outline

Steps to Success

Step 1. Write Outline of Paper
Estimate: Pages, Paragraphs, Main Ideas
- 3 Page Paper has 3 Paragraphs Per Page
- 3 Page Paper has a Total of 9 Paragraphs
- 9 Paragraphs: 1 Main Idea Per Paragraph
- 9 Paragraphs: 7 Main Ideas Plus Intro and Conclusion

The Outline

Page 1
Paragraph 1
Write Introductory Paragraph of Paper
Write a Thesis Statement (point of view to defend).

Paragraph 2
The Most Important Main Idea Is:
Supporting Experts, Quotes, Examples, and Analysis
Citation: Book, Author, Publisher, Copyright, Page #

Paragraph 3
The Second Most Important Main Idea Is:
Supporting Experts, Quotes, Examples, and Analysis
Citation: Book, Author, Publisher, Copyright, Page #

Page 2
Paragraph 4
Main Idea:
Supporting Experts, Quotes, Examples, and Analysis
Citation: Book, Author, Publisher, Copyright, Page #

Paragraph 5
Main Idea:
Supporting Experts, Quotes, Examples, and Analysis
Citation: Book, Author, Publisher, Copyright, Page #

Paragraph 6
Main Idea:
Supporting Experts, Quotes, Examples, and Analysis
Citation: Book, Author, Publisher, Copyright, Page #

Page 3
Paragraph 7
Main Idea:
Supporting Experts, Quotes, Examples, and Analysis
Citation: Book, Author, Publisher, Copyright, Page #

Paragraph 8
Main Idea:
Supporting Experts, Quotes, Examples, and Analysis
Citation: Book, Author, Publisher, Copyright, Page #

Paragraph 9
Write the Concluding Paragraph of Paper
Restate Main Idea and Supporting Ideas and Sum It Up

The Outline
Time Log
Estimate Time: 5 Hours
Actual Time:
Error:
Speedbumps: Any Delays, Detours, and Distractions?

Write Rough Draft of Paper

Tools of the Trade

Write a Thesis Statement
Choose Point of View and Defend Your Position

Use Standard Paper Organization:
Introduction, Body, and Conclusion

Use Standard Paragraph Organization:
Sentence 1. Introductory Sentence
Sentence 2. Expert in Field
Sentence 3. Direct or Indirect Quote
Sentence 4. Examples, Evidence, Explanations
Sentence 5. Analysis (Critical Thinking Tools)
Sentence 6. Concluding Sentence

Use Transitions to Bridge Paragraphs and Ideas
According to, For example, As a result, In conclusion

Apply Critical Thinking Tools (Chapter 10)
Separate Facts from Opinions of Author
Distinguish Theory from Reality

Add Citations: Footnotes or Endnotes
Add Bibliography
Proofread to Perfection (Chapter 9)
Take Control of Your Time with Time Logs
See Teacher for Approval of Rough Draft

Steps to Success

Step 1. Use Standard Paper Format: Introduction, Body, and Conclusion

Step 2. Write the Introduction to Your Paper
Introduce topic, supporting ideas, and include thesis statement.

For Example: Title, Topic, Introduction, Thesis Statement

"The Mountain Lion:
Once Endangered, Now a Danger

On April 23, 1994, as Barbara Schoener was jogging in the Sierra foothills of California, she was pounced on from behind by a mountain lion (Rychnovsky 39). California politicians presented voters with Proposition 197, which contained provisions repealing much of a 1990 law enacted to protect the lions."

Write a Thesis Statement: Take Point of View and Defend
"A future proposition should retain the ban on sport hunting but allow the Department of Fish and Game to control the population. Wildlife management would reduce the number of lion attacks on humans and in the long run would also protect the lions."

Step 3. Write the Body of Your Paper
Follow your Outline and introduce one main idea per paragraph followed by supporting materials of experts in field, direct and indirect quotes, evidence, and sum it up.

Step 4. Write the Conclusion of Your Paper
Restate introduction and main ideas and sum it all up.

The Rough Draft of Paper
Time Log
Estimate Time: 25 Hours
Actual Time:
Error:
Speedbumps: Any Delays, Detours, and Distractions?
Visit Teacher for Approval of Rough Draft

Use Direct and Indirect Quotes

A quotation is a reference to an authority, or a citation of an authority. There are two types of quotations: direct and indirect

Tools of the Trade

Experts in Field
Primary and Secondary Sources
Direct Quotes
Indirect Quotes, Paraphrasing, and Transition Words
Add Citations
Short Quotation Format
Long Quotation Format

You can choose to use either type of quote. Use quotes sparingly. Always provide a context for your quotations that explains to the reader why and how the quote is relevant to the topic.

Choice 1. Direct Quotation

A direct quotation uses the exact words of an authority, and must be documented with quotation marks and a citation.

Choice 2. Indirect Quotation

An indirect quotation, or paraphrase, is a restatement of a thought expressed by someone else that is written in your own words and must be documented with a citation.

Example: Direct Quote

Author John Smith argues that "More people are dying from medical errors than from fatal diseases" (citation).

Example: Indirect Quote (Paraphrase)

According to a recent report, medical errors are killing more people than disease (citation).

Example: Combine Indirect and Direct Quotations

According to a news recent report, medical errors can be fatal as substantiated by the author John Smith, who said, "More people are dying from medical errors than from fatal diseases" (citation).

Example: Use Transition Words for Introductions

You can introduce quotations with transition words, such as, " According to..." or "In sum," as illustrated by the following:

According to Professor John Smith, "add direct quote" (citation).

Professor John Smith **sums up** the situation in the following passage: "add direct quote" (citation).

Example: Short Quotation Format

If your quotations are less than four lines long, place them in your text, and enclose them with quotation marks. This quote begins with an introductory transition word, "According to..."

According to Confucius, "Respect yourself and others will respect you" (citation).

Example: Long Quotation Format

If your quotation is more than four lines long, set it off from your text by indenting. Introduce the quotation with a complete sentence and a colon. Indent ten spaces, double space the lines, and do not use quotation marks.

Confucius sums up the situation in the following passage:

The superior man, when resting in safety, does not forget that danger may come. When in a state of security he does not forget the possibility of ruin. When all is orderly, he does not forget that disorder may come. Thus his person is not endangered, and his States and all their clans are preserved (citation).

Use Direct and Indirect Quotes with Citations
Time Log
Estimate Time: 5 Hours
Actual Time:
Error:
Speedbumps: Any Delays, Detours, and Distractions?

Use Standard Paragraph Formation

Each Paragraph in a Paper is Composed of Five Parts:

Sentence 1   Introductory Sentence and Main Idea

Sentence 2-4   Direct/Indirect Quotes from Experts

Sentence 4-6   Supporting Arguments/Examples

Sentence 6-8   Analysis (Critical Thinking Skills)

Last Sentence   Summation or Concluding Sentence

Step 1. Write the Main Idea Sentence:

According to Professor X ... (direct/indirect quote)

Step 2. Write Supporting Sentences to Defend Your

Position: For example, ...

Step 3. Use Transition Words to Link Ideas

In addition, ...   Furthermore, ...   Moreover,...

Step 4. Write the Analysis Sentences:

As a result, ...

Use **SMARTGRADES** Critical Thinking Tools (Chapter 10)

Step 5. Write Concluding Sentence:

In sum, ...

Use Transition Words

Transition Words Link Ideas Within Paragraphs and Build Bridges Between Paragraphs

Transitions are words and phrases that guide a reader from one idea to the next. Use words sparingly.

To begin a sentence: However, nevertheless, furthermore, therefore

To give examples: As, for example, for instance, In other words, like, such as, that is

For causes: Accordingly, because, due to, for this, for that reason, if ...then, since

For effects: As a result, consequently, for, nevertheless, owing to, so that, therefore, so, thus

For comparisons (similarities): Along with, also, as, besides, both, furthermore, in comparison, in the same way, just as, likewise, moreover, similarly

To add an idea: Again, also, and, furthermore, equally, in addition, moreover

For contrasts (differences): Although, but, by contrast, different from, however, in contrast, instead, nevertheless, on the one hand, on the other hand, rather than, unlike, whereas, yet

For order of importance: All, best, better, first, last, least important, less important, most importantly, most of second, strongest, third, weakest

For temporal order (time): After, as soon as, before, during, finally, first, last, later, meanwhile, next, now, second, since, soon, suddenly, then, third, whenever, while, until, yesterday

For spatial order (place): Above, across, along the side, around, behind, below, beside, center, here, inside, on top of, to the left, in front of, outside, opposite, near, next to, to the center, to the right, there, where

For endings: As a result, finally, in conclusion, in summation

Use Proper Citation Style to Document Sources

Tools of the Trade

MLA Style: Writing in English and Humanities
APA Style: Writing in the Social Sciences
Chicago Style: Writing in History and Humanities

There are two reasons to document your source material:

Reason 1. Show readers where you obtained your facts.

Reason 2. Give readers a list of references should they want to read more about the subject.

Steps to Success

- Cite a source to give the origin of facts or opinions

- Cite a source when using a direct quote

- Cite a source when paraphrasing someone else's work

- Cite a source when stating an unknown fact

- Cite a source when stating controversial facts

Use Citation Format to Document Sources

Tools of the Trade

Footnotes/Endnotes
Parenthetical References

Footnotes and endnotes are basically the same thing — each provides information about where you found the material for your research paper. The only difference is where you put them in your research paper. If you use a quote from a book, you would put a footnote at the bottom (the foot) of the page that the quote appears on, citing the source of the quote. If you're using endnotes instead of footnotes, the endnote would go in a list at the end of the paper with all the other endnotes.

Example: Footnote or Endnote

1- M.I. Finley, "The Silent Women of Rome," in Horizon, no 7 (1965), Tuscaloosa, Horizon Publishers, p. 64.

Parenthetical references are brief citations, enclosed by parentheses, within the text of the paper.

Example: Parenthetical Reference

Shelley thought poets "the unacknowledged legislators of the world" (Magill 2001).

Use Endnotes, Footnotes or Parenthetical References
Time Log
Estimate Time: 5 Hours
Actual Time:
Error:
Speedbumps: Any Delays, Detours, and Distractions?

Write a Bibliography

Tools of the Trade

Author (last name first)
Title of Book
City: Publisher
Date of Publication

Steps to Success

1. For a Book

Author (last name first). Title of the book. City: Publisher, Date of publication.

Example:

Dahl, Roald. The BFG. New York: Farrar, Straus and Giroux, 1982.

2. For an Encyclopedia:

Encyclopedia Title, Edition Date. Volume Number, "Article Title," page numbers.

Example:

The Encyclopedia Britannica, 1997. Volume 7, "Gorillas," pp. 50-51.

3. For a Magazine:

Author (last name first), "Article Title." Name of magazine. Volume number, (Date): page numbers.

Example:

Jordan, Jennifer, "Filming at the Top of the World." Museum of Science Magazine. Volume 47, No. 1, (Winter 1998): p. 11.

4. For a Newspaper:

Author (last name first), "Article Title." Name of newspaper, city, state of publication. (date): edition if available, section, page number(s).

Example:

Powers, Ann, "New Tune for the Material Girl." The New York Times, New York, NY. (3/1/98): Atlantic Region, Section 2, p. 34.

5. For World Wide Web:

URL (Uniform Resource Locator or WWW address). author (or item's name, if mentioned), date.

Example: (Boston Globe's www address)
http://www.boston.com. Today's News, August 1, 1996.

6. For a CD-ROM:

Disc title: Version, Date. "Article title," pages if given. Publisher.

Example:

Compton's Multimedia Encyclopedia: Macintosh version, 1995. "Civil rights movement," p.3. Compton's Newsmedia.

Write Final Draft of Paper

Tools of the Trade

Proofread Paper to Perfection (Chapter 10)

- Check Teacher's Assignment

- Check Paper Content
Q. Does Evidence Support the Thesis Statement?

- Check Paper Structure
Grammar, Spelling, Punctuation, and Neatness

- Hire a Professional Editor to Find Fatal Flaws

- Daily Back Ups on External Hard Drives

Steps to Success

Step 1. Read Assignment Again to Check Requirements
Read assignment sheet again to be sure that you understand fully what is expected of you, and that your essay/research paper meets requirements as specified by your teacher.

Step 2. Let Paper Rest and Read It with Fresh Eyes
If you let the paper sit for a few days, you will later be able to read it from a new perspective and find the remaining flaws, either in structure or content.

Step 3. Use **SMARTGRADES** Proofreading Tools (Chapter 8)

Use proofreading checklist in Chapter 8 (page 169) to correct structural or contextual errors in your paper.

Step 4. Ask a Third Party Editor to Read Your Paper

Find an online editor to read your paper and offer valuable corrections and suggestions. E-mail your paper to the professional editor, and specify a deadline that is at least two weeks before the due-date of your paper. This way, if there is a setback, you will still have time to find another editor in the nick of time to read and correct any fatal flaws.

Step 5. Print Two Copies of Your Paper

Before you hand in your paper to a teacher, make sure that you have a hard copy of your paper in case the teacher misplaces it or loses it (it happens). When your paper is returned to you, throw away your copy.

Step 6. Make Daily Back-Ups on an External Hard Drive

Make sure that you make daily back ups on an external hard drive of the work that is on your computer. There are countless horror stories of students whose computers crashed, and of research papers that were destroyed.

The Final Draft of Paper
Time Log
Estimate Time: 10 Hours
Actual Time:
Error:
Speedbumps: Any Delays, Detours, and Distractions?

EVERY DAY AN EASY A

Checklist to Write an A Grade Paper ☑

☑ **Step 1. The Essay Question**

Q. Did you answer the question asked by restating the essay question as the introductory sentence of your essay?

☑ **Step 2. Thesis Statement**

Q. Did you write a Thesis statement (defend a position)?

☑ **Step 3. Research Topic**

Q. Did you choose a researchable topic?

1. Use encyclopedia for a general overview of topic

2. Find experts in field

3. Read primary source materials (autobiographical)

4. Read secondary source materials (biographical)

5. List pro and con arguments

6. Add direct and indirect quotes from experts

☑ **Step 4. Use Critical Thinking Tools (Chapter 10)**

Q. Did you use your **SMARTGRADES** Critical Thinking Tools to separate facts from opinion of the author?

☑ **Step 5. Write Outline**

Q. Did you write an Outline of the main ideas and supporting examples to properly organize your research?

☑ **Step 6. Use Standard Paper Structure**

Q. Did you use standard paper structure: Introduction, Body, and Conclusion?

☑ **Step 7. Use Standard Paragraph Structure**

Q. Did you use standard paragraph structure: Introductory sentence, quote from expert, supporting examples, analysis, and concluding sentence?

☑ **Step 8. Paraphrase Don't Plagiarize**

Q. Did you paraphrase (write out ideas in your own words)?

☑ **Step 9. Use Transition Words**

Q. Did you use transition words to bridge paragraphs and link ideas within paragraphs? e.g., According to, For example, In addition, As a result, and In conclusion.

☑ **Step 10. Add Citations and Bibliography**

Q. Did you use citations to document your sources?

☑ **Step 11. Proofread Paper to Perfection**

Q. Did you use your **SMARTGRADES SUCCESS STRATEGY** (Chapter 8, Page 169)?

As Long as the World is
Turning and Spinning,
We're Gonna Be Dizzy and
We're Gonna Make Mistakes.

Mel Brooks

Chapter 8, Part II
Proofread Paper to Perfection

Proofread Papers to Perfection

Tools of the Trade

Proofreading to Perfection

- ☐ Time and Patience
- ☐ Enlarging Text
- ☐ Reading Aloud
- ☐ Computer Proofreading Software, e.g., Acrobat

Proofread for Content

- ☐ Check Outline
- ☐ Check Research Material
- ☐ Check Paper Format
- ☐ Check Thesis Statement
- ☐ Check Organization of Ideas
- ☐ Check Redundancy
- ☐ Check Writing Style
- ☐ Check Facts
- ☐ Check Paraphrasing
- ☐ Check Fallacies
- ☐ Check Quotes
- ☐ Check Citation Format

Proofread for Writing Mechanics

- ☐ Check Spelling
- ☐ Check Grammar
- ☐ Check Punctuation
- ☐ Check Paragraph Format
- ☐ Check Sentences
- ☐ Check Word Usage
- ☐ Check Wordiness
- ☐ Check Clichés
- ☐ Check Word Repetition
- ☐ Check Gender
- ☐ Check 3 Nevers
- ☐ Check Neatness

Steps to Success

Step 1. Proofreading Takes Time
Proofreading is a time-intensive task. Set aside at least five to ten hours to read through your paper to proofread it to perfection.

Step 2. Enlarge Text
Your writing software allows you to enlarge the font from 12 to 22 points. You will then be able to see the smallest error, e.g., a comma that is supposed to be a period.

Step 3. Read Aloud
It is easier to find typos when you read your paper aloud. Your ears can find errors that your eyes cannot see.

Step 4. Read Aloud Computer Software
Some computers have speech software programs such as Text Edit or Adobe Acrobat software. These programs will read the paper back to you and locate writing errors.

Proofread for Writing Mechanics

Proofread for Spelling
Q. Did you use computer spellchecker to find spelling errors?

Proofread for Grammar
Q. Did you read for past, present, and future tenses?
Q. Did you keep the tenses in the present tense?

Proofread for Punctuation
Q. Did you check for capitalization of proper nouns, comma overuse, and for periods that stay inside the quotes?

Proofread for Paragraph Format
Q. Did you check for transition words, topic sentence, one main idea per paragraph, supporting examples, quote from expert in the field, analysis that uses your critical thinking skills, and concluding sentence?

Proofread for Sentences
Q. Did you check for sentence fragments, run-ons, or comma splices (change punctuation or add a conjunction).

Proofread for Word Usage
Q. Did you use the thesaurus to find the best word to communicate your ideas and express your exact meaning?

Q. Did you eliminate wordiness?

Q. Did you avoid clichés?

Proofread for Repetition
Q. Did you use the same word over and over again?

Proofread for Gender
Q. Is your use of masculine and feminine pronouns like "he" or "she" appropriate?

Proofread for 3 Nevers
Never begin a sentence with "and" or "because."
Never include personal opinions.
Never use "I" in essays.

Proofread for Neatness
Q. Did you use the correct margins, double spacing, font, and paper?

Proofread for Outline
Q. Does your paper correspond to your original outline?

Proofread for Research
Q. Are your primary and secondary sources credible?

Proofread for Paper Format
Q. Does your paper have an Introduction, Body, and
   Conclusion?

Proofread for Thesis Statement
Q. Is your Thesis clearly stated in your introduction?

Proofread for Organization of Ideas
First give major points, and then give minor points.

Proofread for Redundancy
Q. Did you make the same point more than once?

Proofread for Writing Style
Q. Is your writing style appropriate for the required
   assignment, e.g., creative, scholarly or scientific?

Proofread for Facts
Q. Does your evidence really back up your argument?
   Is all the information relevant to your thesis statement?

Proofread for Paraphrasing
Q. Did you rewrite facts in your own words, and document
   sources?

Proofread for Fallacies (defects that weaken arguments):
Sweeping generalizations, appeal to authority, weak
analogy, or ad populum.

Proofread for Quotes
Q. Are your quotes properly documented in an endnote,
   or in a footnote and in a bibliography?

Proofread for Citation Format
Q. Are your citations correctly formatted: APA, MLA,
   or Chicago

Let's Recap: SMARTGRADES Proofreading Checklist

Q. Did you set aside large blocks of time to proofread your paper to perfection?

Q. Did you enlarge the text to font size 18 to magnify your errors and make them easily visible?

Q. Did you choose font size 18 to find typos?

Q. Did you read your paper out loud to readily weed out all the errors?

Q. Did you purchase speech recognition software to cut in half the time it takes to proofread?

Q. Does paper correspond to your original outline?

Q. Does paper have an Introduction, Body, and Conclusion?

Q. Is your Thesis Statement clearly stated in your introduction?

Q. Is your writing style appropriate for the required assignment, e.g., creative, scholarly, or scientific?

Q. Does your evidence really back up your arguments?

Q. Is all the research relevant to your thesis statement?

Check Paraphrasing

Q. Did you rewrite the facts in your own words, and document the sources?

Check Fallacies (defects that weaken arguments)

(a) Sweeping generalizations

(b) Appeal to authority

(c) Weak analogy

(d) Ad populum

Check Quotes

Q. Are your quotes properly documented in an endnote or in a footnote and in a bibliography?

Check Paragraph Format

Q. Did you check for transition words, topic sentence, one main idea per paragraph, supporting example, quote from expert in the field, analysis and critical thinking skills, and concluding sentence?

Check Sentences

Q. Did you check for sentence fragments, run-ons, or comma splices (change punctuation or add conjunction).

Check Word Usage

Q. Did you use the thesaurus to find the best word to communicate your ideas & express your exact meaning?

Check Neatness

Q. Did you use the correct margins, double spacing, font, and paper?

When You Take a Test,
You Are Really Being
Tested on Two Things:

How Much You Know About the Subject

How Much You Know About Taking a Test

Chapter 9
Read, Memorize, and Test

"If any one faculty of our nature may be called
more wonderful than the rest, I do think it is memory.
There seems something more speakingly
incomprehensible in the powers, the failures,
the inequalities of memory, than in any other of our
intelligences. The memory is sometimes so retentive,
so serviceable, so obedient; at others, so bewildered
and so weak; and at others again, so tyrannic,
so beyond control! We are, to be sure, a miracle
every way; but our powers of recollecting and of
forgetting do seem peculiarly past finding out."

Jane Austen

Chapter 9
Read, Memorize, and Test

Tools of the Trade

Essay Exams

Multiple Choice Exams

True False Exams

Matching Exams

Fill in the Blank Exams

Oral Exams

Open Book Exams

Take Home Exams

Standardized Exams

Steps to Success

Step 1. The Day the Test is Announced

Q. Did you ask the teacher about the test?

a. What subjects are on the test?

b. What subjects are not on the test?

c. How many questions are on the test?

d. How is the test scored?

e. What kind of test is it?

Step 2. Are You Prepared for the Right Type of Test?

a. Essay Exam: Answer the question asked

b. Multiple Choice Exam: The answer is right in front of you

c. Oral Exam: Prepare for a personal interview format

d. Take Home Test: Apply **SMARTGRADES** Critical Thinking Tools for in-depth analysis of the academic material (Chapter 10).

Step 3. Two Weeks Before the Test

Q. Did you review your Test Review Notes? (Chapter 7).

Q. Did you self test to find your strengths and weaknesses?

Q. Did you visit the tutoring center to work out problems?

Q. Did you transform your weaknesses into strengths?

Q. Can you recall the facts for Instant Recall?

Q. Do you remember all of the facts for Total Recall?

Q. Did you change the association cues that do not work?

Step 4. The Night Before the Test

Q. Did you review Test Review Notes for Instant & Total Recall?

Q. Did you get 8 hours of deep sleep to feel energized?

Q. Did you prepare pens, pencils, sharpener, calculator, tissues, and clothing?

Q. Did you set your alarm clock?

Step 5. Manage Your Test Anxiety

Anxiety and stress are debilitating. They will ZAP your energy and destroy your ability to focus and concentrate on the test and you will draw blanks.

Q. Did you practice deep breathing exercises to be
   be able to maintain a calm composure and relax?

The 3-Breath Method of Relaxation Breathing
- Get in a comfortable position, spine straight, feet flat
  on the floor. Close your eyes.
- Concentrate on your body, and notice where there is
  tension, discomfort or stress.
- Take a deep breath, visualize all your stress, then
  breathe out. While breathing out, visualize all the
  stress leaving your body.
- Repeat these steps at least three times.

Step 6. Develop Your Self-Esteem with Positive Self-Talk
Q. When you listen to your inner voice, do you hear
positive supportive messages, e.g.,"I have the strength
to make my dreams come true." On a daily basis, you
need to develop your self-esteem with positive self-talk.

Examples:
- Fear is only a feeling; it cannot hold me back

- I know that my potential is unlimited

- I have the strength to make my dreams come true

- I am proud of myself for even daring to try

- I grow in strength with every forward step I take

- I release my hesitation and make room for victory

Step 7. The Day of the Test

Q. Did you eat right (fiber fuel) for the energy to test?

    a. Breakfast of Champions: Oatmeal with Fresh Fruit

    b. Bran Muffin with Fresh Fruit

Q. Did you review your Test Review Notes to refresh your memory for Instant & Total Recall to ace your test?

The Day Before an Exam:

Prepare for the exam as if you are competing in an athletic event. Be well rested for the mental workout with a good night's sleep. Eat a high energy breakfast at least two hours before the exam, giving enough time for the body to digest the food. The day of the exam warm up the brain with a brief review. Arrive early. Relax. Compose your thoughts. Concentrate. Focus.

1. The Instructions:

First, listen carefully to oral instructions and then read all written instructions.

2. The Test Begins:

Jot down in the corner of the test everything you may forget during the test.

3. The Time:

Budget your time. Do not linger over difficult questions.

4. Your Mental, Emotional, and Spiritual Focus:

Concentrate on what you do know, don't worry about what you don't know.

5. The Question:

- Answer the questions you know first.
- Concentrate on one question at a time.
- Read each question completely before you begin to answer it.
- Answer question asked, not the one you may have expected.
- Go back to the ones you did not answer.
- Don't linger over difficult questions.
- Recall of the information you need may be triggered by completing other questions.

6. The Answer:

- Write down answer before reading choices.
- Read your answer choices carefully.
- Eliminate the choices that are clearly implausible.
- Don't search for hidden or extra meanings.
- Compare similarities & differences between choices.

Examine each word in answer for true or false possibility.
Key Words: All, Only, Always, Because = Generally False
Key Words: Few, Many, Much, Often, Many, Some,
Perhaps, Generally = Possibly True
Break down complex sentences into smaller parts.
If small phrase = false, then entire statement = false.
If each word = false; then entire statement = false.

Change answers if you have a reason for doing so.
However do not change your answers based on a whim.
Use all the time allowed. If you finish early, proofread your paper for errors.

EVERY DAY AN EASY A

How to Ace Your Multiple Choice Test

Steps to Success

Step 1. Answer the easy questions first to build your confidence.

Step 2. Underline the key words in the question and try to answer the question. These tests rely on recognition, rather than recall.

Step 3. Think of multiple choice answers as a series of true or false statements. Read all of the choices even if the first choice seems correct. Compare similarities and differences between choices.

Step 4. Circle the absolute words in the question and the answer.

The absolutes are: all, none, always, never, only. These absolute words usually indicate a false choice.

Step 5. Circle the negative words in the question and the answer. Circle the negative words: not or except. These confusing questions cause careless errors. Mark each option with a T or F. Usually you are looking for a true statement. In this case, you are looking for a false statement.

Step 6. Find the dumb and dumber choices in the answer Cross out the two choices that are dumb and dumber. Examine the question and answer for clues.

Step 7. Change an answer when you have an intelligent reason to do so.

Beware the Dangers of Answer Sheets

Answer sheets allow exams to be scanned and marked automatically. Here are common mistakes to avoid:

1. Remember to record your name and student number on the actual answer sheet.

2. Use pencil so you can correct mistakes.

3. Do not cross out a mistake and mark another answer because the scanner will read this as "two" responses and record it as incorrect.

4. Always check your answers with the right question.

5. Consider marking your answers first on the exam paper, then transferring them to the answer sheet.

EVERY DAY AN EASY A

How to Ace Your Essay Test

Steps to Success

Step 1. Underline Key Word to Answer Question Asked

ANALYZE – Find the main ideas and show how they are related and why they are important.

COMMENT ON – Discuss, criticize, or explain its meaning as completely as possible.

COMPARE – Show both the similarities and differences.

CONTRAST – Show the differences.

CRITICIZE – Give your judgment or reasoned opinion of something, showing its good and bad points. It is not necessary to attack it.

DEFINE – Give the formal meaning by distinguishing it from related terms. This is often a matter of giving a memorized definition.

DESCRIBE – Write a detailed account or verbal picture in a logical sequence or story form.

DIAGRAM – Make a graph, chart, drawing. Be sure you label it and add a brief explanation if it is needed.

DISCUSS – Describe giving the details and explaining the pros and cons of it.

ENUMERATE – Name and list the main ideas one by one. Number them.

EVALUATE – Give your opinion or some expert's opinion of the truth or importance of the concept. Tell the advantages and disadvantages.

ILLUSTRATE – Explain or make it clear by concrete examples, comparison, or analogies.

INTERPRET – Give the meaning using examples and personal comments to make it clear.

JUSTIFY – Give a statement of why you think it is so. Give reasons for your statement or conclusion.

LIST – Produce a numbered list of words, sentences, or comments. Same as enumerate.

OUTLINE – Give a general summary. It should contain a series of main ideas supported by secondary ideas. Omit minor details. Show the organization of the ideas.

PROVE – Show by argument or logic that it is true. The word prove has a very special meaning in mathematics and physics.

RELATE – Show the connections between things, telling how one causes or is like another.

REVIEW – Give a survey or summary in which you look at the important parts and criticize where needed.

STATE – Describe the main points in precise terms. Be formal. Use brief, clear sentences. Omit details or examples.

SUMMARIZE – Give a brief, condensed account of the main ideas. Omit details and examples.

TRACE – Follow the progress or history of the subject.

Step 2. Restate Question as Introductory Sentence
Read the essay question and restate the question as the introductory sentence of your essay and add on the facts.

Example
Q. What are the most important issues your field is facing today?

A. The most important issues that my field is facing today are: Add main ideas and major and minor details.

Step 3. Jot Down Main Ideas and Supporting Details
Jot down in the corner of the test the main ideas and supporting details to organize your thoughts before you write down the answer.

Main Ideas:
1.
2.
3.

Main Idea 1:
Supporting Details:
1. Expert in Field:
2. Indirect Quote:
3. Example:
4. Analysis:
5. Sum It Up:

Main Idea 2:
Supporting Details:
1. Expert in Field:
2. Indirect Quote:
3. Example:
4. Analysis:
5. Sum It Up:

Main Idea 3:
Supporting Details:
1. Expert in Field:
2. Indirect Quote:
3. Example:
4. Analysis:
5. Sum It Up:

Step 4. Use Standard Essay Structure
Use Introduction, Body, and Conclusion

Step 5. Use Standard Paragraph Structure

Sentence 1. Restate essay question ...

Sentence 2. According to Expert... (add quote)

Sentence 3. For example ... (proof)

Sentence 4. As a result ... (analysis)

Sentence 5. In conclusion ... (sum it up)

Step 6. Proofread Paper to Perfection
Proofread for spelling, punctuation, grammar, and neatness.

EVERY DAY AN EASY A

How to Ace Your True False Exam

Steps to Success

Step 1. Examine the Sentence

Every part of a true sentence must be "true." If any one part of the sentence is false, the whole sentence is false despite many other true statements. Long sentences often include groups of words set off by punctuation. Pay attention to the "truth" of each of these phrases. If one is false, it usually indicates a "false" answer.

Step 2. Underline Key Words

Pay close attention to negatives, qualifiers, absolutes, and long strings of statements.

Negatives: "No, Not, Cannot"

Qualifiers: "Sometimes, Often, Frequently, Ordinarily,

Absolutes: : "No, never, none, always, every, entirely, only"

Step 3. Guess True If You Are Unsure

Often true/false tests contain more true answers than false answers. You have more than 50% chance of being right with "true."

How to Ace Your Matching Exam

Steps to Success

Step 1. Use a Light Pencil

Mark them lightly with a pencil until you are completely done.

Step 2. Start with Matches that You Know Instantly

Step 3. Use a Darker Pencil

Make a second pass through matches, mark matches you

are absolutely sure of with a darker penciled line.

Step 4. Search for Clues

Look for clues or relationships in the matches you aren't

100% sure of that you didn't think of the first time.

Step 5. Search for Other Possibilities

Look for another phrase that can be used instead of your

first choice.

EVERY DAY AN EASY A

How to Ace Your Fill in the Blank Exam

Steps to Success

Step 1. The Exam Is the Most Difficult and Most Feared
You have to have the answers, such as names, places, and dates memorized for Instant & Total Recall.

Step 2. SMARTGRADES SUCCESS STRATEGY
Use the new learning technology, **SMARTGRADES SUCCESS STRATEGY** to process (absorb) the facts for Instant & Total Recall and ace the test.

Step 3. Answer the Easy Questions First

Step 4. Underline the Key Words in the Question

Step 5. Other Questions May Jog Your Memory
Sometimes, answers to questions you don't know are supplied in other questions.

Step 6. Educated Guess
The chances of getting a correct answer by writing down a wild guess is very slim, although not entirely unlikely.

How to Ace Your True False Exam

Steps to Success

Step 1. Examine the Sentence

Every part of a true sentence must be "true." If any one
part of the sentence is false, the whole sentence is false,
despite many other true statements. Long sentences
often include groups of words set off by punctuation.
Pay attention to the "truth" of each of these phrases.
If one is false, it usually indicates a "false" answer.

Step 2. Underline Key Words

Pay close attention to negatives, qualifiers, absolutes,
and long strings of statements.

Negatives: "No, Not, Cannot"

Qualifiers: "Sometimes, Often, Frequently, Ordinarily,

Absolutes: "No, never, none, always, every, entirely, only"

Step 3. Guess True If You Are Unsure

Often true/false tests contain more true answers than
false answers. You have more than 50% chance of being
right with "true."

How to Ace Your Open Book Exam

Steps to Success

Step 1. Use Textbook and Test Review Notes
Since you have already condensed the facts from your textbook into Test Review Notes, they are probably the fastest way to access the facts.

Step 2. Use Standard Essay Format
a. Write in complete sentences.
b. Restate the essay question as the introductory sentence and add on the facts.
c. Use an Introduction, Body, and Conclusion
d. Use transition words to bridge ideas:

Sentence 1. On one hand ... (the Pro argument)
           On the other hand ... (the Con argument)
Sentence 2. According to expert... (add quote)
Sentence 3. For example ...
Sentence 4. As a result ... (analysis)
Sentence 5. In conclusion ... (sum it up)

Step 3. Proofread to Perfection
Check for spelling, grammar, punctuation, and neatness.

How to Ace Your Take Home Exam

Steps to Success

Step 1. What Kinds of Material Can Be Used?

Take Home exams are unrestricted. The main restriction for Take Home exams is that they must be your work–you must attempt them by yourself without any help from others.

Step 2. What Do Take Home Exams Test?

They don't test your memory. They test your ability to find and use information for problem solving, and to deliver well-structured and well-presented arguments and solutions. They require you to apply knowledge rather than just remember facts.

Step 3. Follow the Instructions for Open Book Exams

Step 4. Use SMARTGRADES Critical Thinking Tools

To give a comprehensive analysis of the academic material, apply all of the **SMARTGRADES** Critical Thinking Tools found in Chapter 10.

EVERY DAY AN EASY A

How to Ace Your Oral Exam

Steps to Success

Step 1. Create a Good Impression

- Dress well and appropriately

- Turn off your cell phone

- Arrive at the location early

- Review Test Review Notes

- Practice positive self-talk: "I am the brightest banana in the bunch."

Step 2: Oral Exams Are Similar to Interviews

- Introduce yourself immediately and smile

- Give the instructor all of your attention

- Keep good posture and eye contact

- Stay focused through the exam

- Maintain your self-confidence and composure

- Be an intelligent listener as well as a talker

- Do not ramble if you do not know an answer

- If you do not know the answer, ask the teacher to ask the question in a different format to jog your memory

- Answer questions with more than "yes" or "no"

- Use two or three key points or examples to demonstrate your knowledge

- Thank the instructor

How to Transform an Exam Failure into a Success

You rushed through an exam, afraid that you will run out of time, and made careless mistakes:

- You misread the questions

- You misread the directions

- You blackened the wrong box on an answer sheet

- You skipped a question or two

- You forgot to write legibly

Steps to Success

Step 1. Ask for a Redo
An instructor may allow you to rewrite an essay exam, rework a math problem from the original question, and improve your grade. The worst they are going to say is no.

Step 2. Ask for Extra Credit Work
Ask for extra credit work to make up for a poor performance on a key exam.

Step 3. Review Mistakes
All knowledge bases are cumulative. Sometimes you get a problem wrong because you didn't understand the subject as well as you thought. After an exam fill in your knowledge gaps, to be prepared for the next test.

Step 4. Talk to Your Teacher
Ask your instructor for an explanation of your grade or comment. Use this as a time to find out how you can do better next time. Keep track of your strengths and weaknesses.

Standardized Exam Tools
How to Ace Your Verbal Analogy Exam

Steps to Success

Step 1. First, create a sentence in your mind that uses the two capitalized words.

Step 2. Learn to recognize common types of analogies.

Step 3. Eliminate answer pairs that are clearly wrong.

Step 4. Beware of possibly correct answers that appear in reverse order.

Step 5. If more than one choice appears possible, analyze the words again.

Step 6. Consider alternative meanings of words, as well as alternative parts of speech.

Step 7. If you don't know the meaning a word, try to recall if you've ever heard it in an expression. The context of the expression may suggest the meaning of the word.

Step 8. Beware of obvious answers. They may be there only to mislead you.

Standardized Exam Tools
How to Ace Your Verbal Antonyms Exam

Steps to Success

Step 1. Use word parts (prefixes, roots, suffixes) to figure out the probable meaning of unknown words.

Step 2. Be aware of secondary meanings of words. For example, 'appreciation' can just as readily mean 'increase' as it does 'gratitude'. When no answer seems correct, look for an alternative (or 'secondary') meaning for your antonym/opposite choice.

Step 3. Consider the 'feel' of the word. It may create a sense in you of its meaning, such as a word like 'grandiose'. It may have a positive or negative connotation, which may help you to eliminate some choices.

Step 4. Try to think of similarly constructed words that you may recognize and that may give you a clue as to the meaning of an otherwise unknown word.

Step 5. Think of a recognizable context for a word you don't recognize. Let the context of the word in a phrase or sentence suggest its probable meaning.

Step 6. Think of an opposite meaning for the capitalized word, even before you look at the actual choices.

Step 7. Read all the choices before selecting your answer.

What Is the Hardest Task in the World?
To Think.

Ralph Waldo Emerson

Chapter 10
Critical Thinking Tools

Aristotle's Topoi

1. Use Definition
2. Explore Relationship
3. Examine Circumstance
4. Rely on Testimony

Aristotle, one of the fathers of rhetoric, asked a series of questions that might lead you to interesting paper topics.

The Trouble with the World
Is that the Stupid Are Cocksure and
the Intelligent Are Full of Doubt.

Bertrand Russell

Sharon Esther Lampert

Chapter 10
Critical Thinking Tools

Tools of the Trade

1. Read with an Open Mind

2. Read with a Critical Mind

3. Evaluate the Underlying Assumptions

4. Read for Arguments Based on Fallacies

5. Read for Inductive and Deductive Reasoning

Steps to Success

Step 1. Read with an Open Mind

Develop mental flexibility, a willingness to think clearly and weigh all sides of every question. To resolve a problem, attack a problem with an open mind. Prepare to consider all possibilities and probe the issue to the heart.

Step 2. Read with a Critical Mind

Separate the facts of the story (verifiable evidence) from the opinions of the author. Caution: Some facts, such as statistical surveys and historical events are based on "opinions."

Step 3. Evaluate the Underlying Assumptions
Assumptions are the set of belief systems that are considered to be self-evident.

Step 4. Read for Arguments Based on Fallacies
Learn to recognize the presentation of misleading evidence that is false.

Misdirected Appeals: Appeal to authority, appeal to common or popular belief, appeal to common practice or tradition, appeal to indirect consequences, appeal to wishful thinking.

Emotional Appeals: Appeal to fear or scare tactics, appeal to force, appeal to loyalty or peer pressure, appeal to pity or sob story, appeal to prejudice, appeal to stereotypes, appeal to hatred, appeal to vanity.

Step 5. Read for Inductive and Deductive Reasoning
Induction argues from observation from the specific to the general. Deduction argues from the general to the specific (rules and laws).

A Checklist for Critical Thinking Tools

Q1. Did you read with an open mind?

Q2. Did you think clearly and weigh all sides of every question?

Q3. Did you resolve a problem, and attack a problem with a flexible mind?

Q4. Did you consider all possibilities and probe the issue to the heart?

Q5. Did you read with a critical mind and separate the facts of the story (verifiable evidence) from the opinions of the author.

Q6. Did you evaluate the underlying assumptions?

Q7. Did you read for arguments based on fallacies?

Misdirected Appeals:
1. Appeal to authority
2. Appeal to common or popular belief
3. Appeal to common practice or tradition
4. Appeal to indirect consequences
5. Appeal to wishful thinking

Emotional Appeals:
1. Appeal to fear or scare tactics
2. Appeal to force
3. Appeal to loyalty or peer pressure
4. Appeal to pity or sob story
5. Appeal to prejudice
6. Appeal to stereotypes
7. Appeal to hatred
8. Appeal to vanity

Q. Did you read for inductive and deductive reasoning?

If I Create from the Heart,
Nearly Everything Works;
If from the Head Almost Nothing!
Marc Chagall

Critical Thinking	**Creative Thinking**
analytic	generative
convergent	divergent
vertical	lateral
probability	possibility
judgment	suspended judgment
focused	diffuse
objective	subjective
answer	answers
left brain	right brain
verbal	visual
linear	associative
reasoning	richness, novelty
yes but	yes and

Chapter 11
WORLD PREMIERE!

10 Esoteric Laws of Creativity

POE**T**REE

Ink needs a pen.
Pen needs paper.
Paper needs a poem.
Poem needs a poet.
Poet needs a muse.
Muse needs a poet.
Poet needs divine inspiration.
Divine inspiration needs divine intervention.
Divine intervention needs divine grace.
Divine grace needs immortality.
Immortality needs eternity.
Eternity needs readers of poetry.

Sharon Esther Lampert
V.E.S.S.E.L.: VERY. EXTRA. SPECIAL. SHARON. ESTHER. LAMPERT.

"Please Handle My Poems Gently.
These Poems Are My Remains."

Sharon Esther Lampert

www.WorldFamousPoems.com
The Greatest Poems Ever Written on Extraordinary World Events

Chapter 11
WORLD PREMIERE!
Creative Thinking Tools

10 Tools of the Trade

1. V.E.S.S.E.L.

2. INSPIRATION

3. IMPREGNATION

4. INCUBATION

5. GENESIS

6. SILENT:LISTEN

7. METAMORPHOSIS

8. REVELATION

9. SIGNATURE

10. IMMORTALITY

Read: "Unleash The Creator, The God Within:
10 Esoteric Laws of Genius & Creativity"

Steps to Success

Step 1. V.E.S.S.E.L.
Keep an open mind and heart, so that you can receive inspirations that come from everywhere. Artistic gifts are inherited. There are good, great, and gifted **ARTISTS.**

Step 2. INSPIRATION
When something moves you emotionally, and transforms your inner world in such a way that you feel differently, think differently, and see differently — that external force is called inspiration. Inspiration is everywhere!

Step 3. IMPREGATION (ARTIST & ARTWORK BECOME ONE)
You are inspired and become impregnated with an idea.

Step 4. INCUBATION
The **ARTWORK** resides within the **ARTIST** and grows quietly over time.There is no such thing as "Writer's Block." It is a myth. You must be patient and allow **ARTWORK** to incubate within you.

Step 5. GENESIS (ARTIST & ARTWORK BECOME TWO)
When **ARTWORK** is ready to be born, it takes on a life of its own, separates from the **ARTIST**, and has its own destiny (mission, message, and meaning) e.g., music composition.

Step 6. SILENT: LISTEN
The **ARTIST** remains silent and listens within to the **ARTWORK**.

Step 7. METAMORPHOSIS: MISSION, MEANING, MESSAGE
The **ART** and the **ARTIST** are now two separate entities. The **ART** and the **ARTIST** have to be nurtured for both of them to grow and reach maturity.

Step 8. REVELATION: MESSAGE
The **ART** touches other people with its own message, and has its distinct own destiny, separate from the **ARTIST**.

Step 9. SIGNATURE
The **ART** bears the autograph of the **ARTIST**.

Step 10. IMMORTALITY
ARTWORK lives beyond the life of the **ARTIST**.
ARTIST IS MORTAL. ART IS IMMORTAL.

Steps to Success

Most creative people credit their vivid imaginations
for their success, e.g., J.K. Rowling's Harry Potter.

Q1. Do you have the emotional, spiritual, and intellectual
fortitude to express your ideas without fear from shame
and ridicule?

Q2. Do you have a vivid imagination?

Q3. Do you write down your wild'n'crazy ideas and let
them mature into a poem, a play, or a novel?

Q4. Are you a daydreamer? Do you write down your
daydreams?

Q5. Do you let your mind flow freely to associate and
brainstorm for ideas?

To Do List: Creative Idea Journal

Creative thinking requires thinking "outside the box."

Start a creative ideas journal. List all ideas that come to
mind, no matter how bizarre, weird, or strange, and see
where they take you. Perhaps a novel will emerge, or
a poem, or a plot for a movie script or even a play.

Research Is What I'm Doing
When I Don't Know What I'm Doing

Wernher Von Braun

I Would Rather Have
Questions That Can't Be Answered
Then Answers Which Can't Be Questioned

Richard Feynman

Chapter 12
Scientific Thinking Tools

EVERY DAY AN EASY A

Chapter 12
Scientific Thinking Tools

The scientific method is a process for experimentation that is used to explore observations that use the five senses, and to answer questions about the natural world. Scientists use the scientific method to search for cause and effect relationships in nature. An experiment is designed so that changes to one item cause something else to vary in a predictable way. The sciences rely heavily on numbers as data, and on replicable experimentation to measure and calculate results.

Tools of the Trade

The Scientific Method

- Make Observations By Using Your 5 Senses
- Ask Questions
- Perform Experiments
- Collect Data
- Measure Data
- Classify Data
- Make a Hypothesis
- Interpret Data
- Analyze Information
- Draw Conclusions
- Make a Prediction
- Verification of Experiment

The Science Report

Q: What Is Scientific Thinking?

Scientific (and critical) thinking is based on three things:

1. **Empiricism:** Using empirical evidence found in nature. Using evidence that is found in nature. It is evidence that is perceptible from the senses; evidence that one can see, hear, touch, taste, or smell.

2. **Rationalism:** Practicing logical reasoning

3. **Skepticism:** Possessing a skeptical attitude about presumed knowledge that leads to self-questioning, holding tentative conclusions, and being undogmatic (willingness to change one's beliefs).

WORLD PEACE EQUATION

VG+VL=VP

Virtue of the Good + Value of Life = Vision of Peace

The Mathematical and Philosophical Proof for World Peace

$$VG + VL = VP$$
$$VP = VG + VL$$
$$VP = V(G+L)$$
$$P = (G+L)$$
$$Peace = Good + Life$$
$$Peace = Goodlife$$

PHOTON
SUPERHERO OF EDUCATION
www.BooksNotBombs.com

Chapter 13
Mathematical Thinking Tools

The Highest Form of Pure Thought Is in Mathematics

Plato
Ancient Greek Philosopher
428 BC-348 BC

Chapter 13
Mathematical Thinking Tools

Math is learned by solving many types of problems. Math is cumulative. Every class builds on the previous one.

Tools of the Trade

Solving Math Problems

1. Think in steps: Step by step
2. Memorize the fundamentals
3. Translate abstract concepts into concrete terms

Ask Questions

1. What is given?
2. What is called for?
3. How many steps are required?
4. What operation must be used in each step?
5. Are the steps in the right order?
6. Check answer and make sure it is right

Math Errors

20% of All Math Errors Are Careless Mistakes

1. Write each number legibly
2. Place two columns of figures exactly under one another
3. Copy each problem correctly

Steps to Success

In-Class Math Strategy: Take Organized Math Notes
Keep a list of the types of math problems solved and the
sequence of steps:

Math Problem Type   Equations Used   Sequence of Steps

- As questions arise, ask your teacher for clarification.
- Don't leave class feeling lost, confused, and hopeless.

At-Home Math Strategy: Rework Class Problems
After every class, review your class notes and rework
the math problems covered in class

Step 1. Write Out the Math Problem
- Read the word problem slowly and carefully.

- Remember this adage: Go slow to go fast.

- Slow is the way to accuracy and great grades.

- Write out the problem, number the steps, and double
  check what you've written.

- What are you trying to figure out? The last sentence of
  a word problem tells you what you are trying to find.

Step 2. Write Down the Information in the Problem

Data   **Variable**   **Equation**

Word problems contain all the information needed to answer the question.

- List all the information given in the problem.

- Make two lists: Separate the knowns from the unknowns (the variable).

Knowns   **Unknowns**

Q. What is the relationship between the known and the unknown values?

- Write an equation.

- Solve for the unknowns.

Step 3. What is the Best Math Method?
Make a plan and solve the problem. Develop a plan to solve the problem and solve it according to your plan.

Q1. How many steps does it take to solve the problem?

Q2. Does one part of the problem have to be solved before other parts can be solved?

Q3. Can the problem be divided into parts and solved separately?

Step 4. Check Your Work and Reread the Problem

- Check to see that you did not leave out any steps of your plan.

- Read problem again to see if your answer makes sense.

- Check answers for careless mistakes.

- Double check your calculator work immediately.

Step 5. Math Test Success Strategy

- Solve unassigned homework problems and see if you can finish them in the allotted time for the exam.

- Write big and bold. This will allow you to see a mistake and keep from confusing numbers, letters, or signs. Careless errors often creep in because you don't give yourself enough space to see and solve the problem.

- Answer the easy questions first to build your confidence. Budget your time.

- If you get stuck on a problem move on and come back to it later.

- Don't leave if you finish the exam early. Go back to the difficult problems.

- Use all of the available time to look for careless errors.

If You Think Dogs Can't Count,
Try Putting Three Dog Biscuits in Your
Pocket, and Then Giving Fido
Only Two of Them.

Phil Pastoret

Little Johnny

Little Johnny was sitting in class doing math problems when his teacher picked him to answer a question, "Johnny, if there were five birds sitting on a fence and you shot one with your gun, how many would be left?" "None," replied Johnny, "cause the rest would fly away." "Well, the answer is four," said the teacher, "but I like the way you're thinking."

We Receive Three Educations,
One from Our Parents,
One from Our Schoolmasters,
and One From the World.
The Third Contradicts All
that the First Two Teach Us

Charles Louis de Secondat, Baron de Montesquieu

Chapter 14
Summer Internship, Life Experience, Network, and Career Choices

NEW PROGRAM
How to Get Into Medical School
Without Hard Sciences

Humanities and Medicine Program at the
Mount Sinai Medical School on the
Upper East Side of Manhattan
35 Undergraduate Slots a Year
Program Director: Dr. Nathan Kase

Follow Your Passion,
Fulfill Your Potential, and
Find Your Place in the World

PHOTON

SUPERHERO OF EDUCATION
EVERYBODY IS SOMEBODY SPECIAL
www.PhotonSuperhero.com

Chapter 14
Summer Internship, Life Experience, and Network

Once you find your passion, it is time to pursue a summer internship in that field. If you start early, you may even find a paid internship that may lead to full time employment after you graduate.

If you are still undecided, then it is best to make a list of possibilities and pursue a summer internship in a field that is interesting to you.

1st Choice: Film and Television (major in arts)
2nd Choice: Accountant (practical minor)
3rd Choice: Start my own internet business

There are countless medical students who found out late in the game that they do not like being doctors. There are countless lawyers who found out late in the game that the legal profession was a mistake. Use the summer to explore your career interests to see whether you are on the right career path.

Make a list of the interesting people in your field who inspire you. Write each one a letter and let them know that you are looking for a summer position as an intern.

The most important benefit of working as a summer intern is that they may offer you a full time job after you graduate.

The Game Plan: My Summer Internship
- ☐ Step 1. Make a list of the people that inspire you
- ☐ Step 2. Research the company
- ☐ Step 3. Write a letter
- ☐ Step 4. Contact company for internships
- ☐ Step 5. The summer internship
- ☐ Step 6. Full time job after graduation

Dear ....

I admire and respect the work that you do . . .

I am interested in applying for a summer internship position in your company. . .

I believe that I would be an asset . . .

Thank you for your consideration.

Sincerely,

Signature

Networking

Stay in touch with people you admire even if they can't help you immediately.

Step 1. Read an article written by an expert that you respect.

Step 2. Write a letter to that person and comment on the article.

Step 3. Let that person know that you are a student and would like to work in the same field.

Step 4. Ask for advice as to how best to pursue a career along the same path.

Step 5. Print some business cards to enclose in your letters or to hand out when you are out and about net working at an event. Choose a card that has color and design with personality.

<table>
<tr><td>
My First Business Card (add logo)
Name
Phone
E-mail
Website
</td></tr>
</table>

Step 6. Send that person regular updates of articles and sign them, "Thinking of You."

Step 7. Ask if you could interview the person for the student club newsletter to meet he/she in person.

EVERY DAY AN EASY A

How to Choose a Career That Fits Your Personality Type

Read through the lists below for careers that are interesting to you and that will need futher exploration to acertain whether you are well suited based on your intellectual and emotional strengths and weaknesses.

Hands-On Career Choices (for the physically active)
Air Traffic Controller, Archaeologist, Athletic Trainer, Carpenter, Caterer, Cartographer, Chef, Computer Repairs Engineer Construction Worker, Dental Technician, Drafter, Electrician, Farm Manager, Firefighter, Fish and Game Warden, Forester, Hairdresser, Landscape Architect, Licensed Practical Nurse, Locksmith, Mechanic, Machinist, Military Officer, Physical Therapist, Police Officer, Plumber, Recreation Administrator, Surveyor, Teacher, Truck Driver, X-Ray Technician

Helper Career Choices
(working with people, good communicators)
Airline Personnel, Athletic Coach, Attorney, Career Counselor, Chamber of Commerce Claims Adjuster, Child Care Worker, Cosmetologist, Counselor, Dietitian, Fitness Instructor, Funeral Director, Home Health Aide, Information Clerk, Occupational Therapist, Mental Health Specialist, Nurse, Office Worker Paramedic, Parole Officer, Personnel Director, Physical Therapist, Receptionist, Recreation Director, Religious Worker, Teacher, Therapist, Travel Agent, Sales Representative, Social Worker, Waiter/Waitress, Youth Service Worker

Investigator Career Choices
(curious, logical, think independently, work alone)
Astronomer, Biologist, College Professor, Computer Analyst, Computer System Analyst, Consumer Researcher, Dentist, Dietitian, Ecologist, Engineer, Horticulturist, Lawyer, Librarian, Medical Technologist, Meteorologist, Nurse, Paralegal, Pharmacist, Physician, Police Detective, Reporter, Research Analyst, Science Lab Technician, Science/Math Teacher, Technical Writer, Veterinarian

Helper Career Choices
(working with people, good communicators)
Airline Personnel, Athletic Coach, Attorney Career Counselor, Chamber of Commerce Claims Adjuster, Child Care Worker, Cosmetologist, Counselor, Dietitian, Fitness Instructor, Funeral Director, Home Health Aide Information Clerk, Occupational Therapist Mental Health Specialist, Nurse, Office Worker Paramedic, Parole Officer, Personnel Director Physical Therapist, Receptionist, Recreation Director, Religious Worker, Teacher, Therapist, Travel Agent, Sales Representative, Social Worker, Waiter/Waitress, Youth Service Worker

Enterprise Career Choices
(outgoing, self-confident, sociable, adventurous)
Advertising Agent, Advertising Executive, Announcer, Banker, Business Manager, Campaign Manager, Entrepreneur, Florist, Insurance Manager, Lawyer, Lobbyist, Office Manager, Personnel Recruiter, Police Officer, Politician, Real Estate Appraiser, Sales Person, Stock Broker, Travel Agent, TV/Radio

Artist Career Choices
(self-expression, imaginative, innovative)

Advertising Manager, Architect, Artist, Cartographer, Cosmetologist, Dance Instructor, Drama Coach, English Teacher, Entertainer, Florist, Graphic Designer, Interior Decorator, Illustrator, Journalist, Landscaper, Librarian, Lighting Specialist, Museum Curator, Music Teacher, Musician, Painter, Photographer Recording Technician, Reporter, Writer

Science Career Choices
(curious, logical, think independently, work alone)

Aerospace Engineer, Astronomer, Aviation Inspector, Athletic Trainer, Biochemist, CAD Technician, Chemist, Civil Engineer, Computer Hardware Engineer, Computer Programmer, Computer Software Engineer, Diver, Electrical Engineer Electrician, Environmental Engineer, Food Science Technician Food Scientist or Technologist, Genetic Counselor, Geographer, Geologist, Industrial Engineer, Marine Architect, Mechanical Engineer, Medical and Clinical Laboratory Technician, Meteorologist, Microbiologist, Multi-Media Artist or Animator, Natural Sciences Manager, Physicist, Pilot, Plant Scientist, Psychologist, Ship and Boat Captain, Sociologist, Sound Engineering Technician, Statistician, Veterinarian, Zoologist, Wildlife Biologist.

Detailers Career Choices
(steady routines, defined procedures, collecting and organizing)

Accountant, Actuary, Administrative Assistant, Auditor Statistician, Bank Manager, Business Teacher, Librarian, Bookkeeper, Cartographer, Cashier, Credit Manager, CAD Operator, Coat Analyst, Corrections Officer, Computer Operator, Court Reporter, Estimator, Financial Analyst, Hotel Clerk, Insurance Underwriter, Medical Lab Technologist, Medical Secretary, Personnel Clerk, Secretary, Paralegal, Proofreader, Reservations Agent, Safety Inspector, Tax Consultant

Know Thyself

1. What type of career is best suited to your personality type?

2. What are your strengths and weaknesses?

3. What social causes are you most concerned about?

4. If you could change something in the world, what would it be?

5. Where do you think you can make a difference?

Obstacles Are those Frightful Things You See
When You Take Your Eyes Off Your Goal

Henry Ford

Chapter 15
Graduate, Resume, Interview, Job

Choose a Job You Love, and You Will
Never have to Work a Day in Your Life

Confucius

Chapter 15
Graduate, Resume, Interview, Job

Make a list of the online job websites that are in your chosen field, and sign up as a job seeker. Explore the jobs offered and check out the companies offering jobs that are of interest to you. Examine the qualifications required for the jobs, as this may help you choose courses that are relevant to a future employer.

Start working on your cover letter and resume to find your own style of writing that will give you a competitive edge in the marketplace.

Q. What kind of resume will work best for you?
1. Chronological Resume
   A chronological resume lists your work history, with the most recent position listed first.

2. Functional Resume
   A functional resume focuses on your skills and experience than on your chronological work history.

3. Combination Resume

A combination resume lists your skills and experience first. Your employment history is listed next.

4. Targeted Resume

A targeted resume specifically highlights the experience and skills you have that are relevant to the job you are applying for.

5. Mini Resume

A mini resume contains a brief summary of your career highlights and qualifications.

Resume Action Words

Use verbs to describe your skills and accomplishments.

1. Communication/People Skills
2. Creative Skills
3. Data/Financial Skills
4. Helping Skills
5. Management/Leadership Skills
6. Organizational Skills
7. Research Skills
8. Teaching Skills
9. Technical Skills

1. Communication/People Skills

Addressed, Advertised, Arbitrated, Arranged, Articulated, Authored, Clarified, Collaborated, Communicated

2. Creative Skills

Acted, Adapted, Began, Combined, Composed, Conceptualized, Condensed, Created, Customized

3. Data/Financial Skills

Administered, Adjusted, Allocated, Analyzed, Appraised, Assessed, Audited, Balanced, Budgeted, Calculated

4. Helping Skills

Adapted, Advocated, Aided, Answered, Arranged, Assessed, Assisted, Clarified, Coached, Collaborated

5. Management/Leadership Skills

Administered, Analyzed, Appointed, Approved, Assigned, Attained, Authorized, Chaired, Considered, Consolidated

6. Organizational Skills

Approved, Arranged, Catalogued, Categorized, Charted, Classified, Coded, Collected, Compiled, Corrected

7. Research Skills

Analyzed, Clarified, Collected, Compared, Conducted, Critiqued, Detected, Determined, Diagnosed, Evaluated

8. Teaching Skills

Adapted, Advised, Clarified, Coached, Communicated, Conducted, Coordinated, Critiqued, Developed, Enabled

9. Technical Skills

Applied, Assembled, Built, Calculated, Computed, Conserved, Constructed, Converted, Debugged, Designed

Q. How Do People Get Jobs?

- Apply for an advertised job

- Internal promotion

- Word of mouth

- Nepotism (personal connections)

- Going through an agency or using head hunters

- Identifying a company you want to work for, and being pro-active about getting through the door.

Your First Interview:

- People decide about you in the first 10 seconds

- Wear suitable interview clothes

- Take copies of your resume with you

- Arrive on time for your job interview

- Always greet the interviewer by his/her last name

- Have a good firm handshake

- Look alert and interested

- Keep your eyes on the interviewer

- Wait until you are offered a chair before you sit down

- Stress your achievements

- Be enthusiastic and show it in your body language

- Answer the interview question by more than a simple yes or no, but try not to go over the 60 second limit

- Don't complain about your current employer

- Do not answer questions about politics or religion

- Do not raise salary discussions on your first interview

- Send a thank you letter

Learn as much as you can about the company:

Q1. What does their website tell you about them?

Q2. Why do you want to work for them?

Q3. Think about what they need

Q4. Who are their competitors?

Q5. Are they well established?

Q6. What do you want to know about them?

Q7. What do you like about them?

Prepare answers for the classic interview questions:

Q1. Tell me about yourself

Q2. What have you been doing lately?

Q3. What made you apply for this job?

Q4. Why should we pick you?

Q5. What attracted you to our company?

Q6. Why are you leaving your current job?

Q7. Why do you want to work for this company?

Q8. What do you see as your strengths and weaknesses?

Q9. How do you see yourself in 5 years time?

Q10. How do you like to work?

Q11. What can you bring to the company?

Q12. Why should we employ you?

Q13. What do you do outside work?

Here are some questions to ask the employer:

Q1. What's the most important quality you're looking for?

Q2. Why do you think people like working here?

WHAT DIFFERENT DEGREES MEAN

The graduate with a science degree asks,
"Why does it work?"

The graduate with an engineering degree asks,
"How does it work?"

The graduate with a management degree asks,
"How much will it cost?"

The graduate with an arts degree asks,
"Do you want fries with that?"

COLLEGE LIFE

University Grading Systems

DEPT OF STATISTICS
All grades are plotted along the Normal (Gaussian) curve.

DEPT OF PSYCHOLOGY
Students are asked to blot ink in their exam books, close them, and turn them in. The professor opens the books and assigns the first grade that comes to mind.

DEPT OF HISTORY
All students get the same grade they got last year.

DEPT OF RELIGION
Grade is determined by God.

DEPT OF PHILOSOPHY
What is a grade?

LAW SCHOOL
Students are asked to defend their position of why they should receive an A.

COLLEGE LIFE

Tools of the Trade

Dorm Room Etiquette
Just Rommates
How to Get Along with Your Roommate
How to Mediate a Roommate Dispute
How to Do Your Own Laundry
How to Solve a SUDUKO Puzzle

Steps to Success

Dorm Room Etiquette

1. Call the school and find out how early you can move in
   to your dorm room. Move in early to choose the best bed
   and closet space available, and to avoid the chaotic
   atmosphere.

2. Find out if you are allowed to own a hot pot, mini
   refrigerator, or microwave before you pack them.

3. Contact your roommate ahead of time to find out what
   he or she plans to bring. Make sure you are not
   duplicating large items such as televisions or stereos.

4. Bring mostly casual wear for studying. Do not bring
   clothing that needs ironing, or fabrics that will shrink
   in the dryer.

Dorm Room Packing Checklist

Bring an Alarm Clock ☐

Q. What does your roomate prefer to wake-up to, noise or music? If music, what kind of music? Work it out!

Bathroom Supplies

- Bathrobe ☐
- Towels for Bath and Face (30 Day Supply) ☐
- Soap ☐
- Toilet Paper ☐
- Tissues ☐
- Shampoo and Conditioner ☐
- Razor and Shaving Cream ☐
- Hairdryer and Brush ☐
- Tampons and Napkins ☐
- Contraception, e.g., Condoms, Birth Control Pills ☐
- Cleaning Supplies for Tile, Mirror, and Laundry ☐
- Laundry Bag ☐

Bedding Supplies

- Pillow and Blankets (light and heavy) ☐
- Pack 4 Sets of Sheets (to postpone laundry) ☐

Clothing Supplies

Bring 30 days of underwear, socks and T-shirts so that you can postpone having to do a laundry for a month.

- 30 Days of Underwear and Socks ☐
- 30 Days of T-shirts ☐
- Pants: Jeans ☐

Exercise Clothing

- Sweats ☐
- Jogging Outfits ☐
- Weight Lifting Gloves ☐
- Swimwear ☐
- Gym Bag ☐

Footwear

- Daily Shoes ☐
- Dressy Shoes ☐
- Sneakers ☐
- Bedroom Slippers ☐
- Shower Thongs (to avoid slippery floor) ☐
- Rainboots and Umbrella ☐

Outer Wear

- Wintercoat ☐
- Raincoat ☐
- Sweaters ☐

Computer Equipment (pack computer carefully)

- Computer and Printer ☐
- External Hard Drive for Daily Backups ☐
- Computer Ink ☐
- Computer Paper ☐
- Extention Cord ☐
- Power Strip ☐
- Desk Lamp and Lightbulbs ☐
- Bring Photos of Loved Ones for Desk ☐

Just Roommates

Don't assume that you and your roommate will become friends. In most college roommate scenarios, you will probably be roommates and have little else in common. There will be chasms of social, cultural, religious, and political differences between the two of you, and closeness might only intensify the differences and generate interpersonal conflict. In addition, college is a competitive atmosphere, and competitive isolation is the norm. Set some personal boundaries in case the two of you are completely mismatched. For example, you are a nerd and can't get a date, and your roommate is a jock and the fans flock like feathers. Or you are still a virgin, and your roomate is engaged to be married. As in most situations, hope for the best, but prepare for the worst.

How to Get Along with Your Roommate

- Always ask before you borrow anything, even if you have borrowed it before.

Bathroom Policy

You will be sharing a bathroom, so establish some guidelines:

Q. What time will you use the shower?

Q. What day of the week do we clean the bathroom?

Q. How will the cost of toilet paper, cleaning supplies, and light bulbs be decided?

Q. How will you divide up the towel racks?

Q. Where will you keep your shampoo, soap, and toothbrush?

Guest Policy

Decide when the room is on and off limits to family members and guests who want to visit and hang out.

Cleaning Policy

Make a list of what needs to be cleaned, how often, and how the chores will be divided.

1. Floor
2. Windows
3. Mirror
4. Bathroom
5. Garbage pails in the bathroom and bedroom

Q. Will you divide up the chores or take turns?

Smoking, Drinking, Drugs, and Sex Policy

Discuss whether the dorm room is off limits for smoking, alcohol, and sexual encounters.

How to Mediate a Roommate Dispute

There will be some disagreement or problem that will need to be resolved. Try to deal with it in a civilized way.

Plan A: Agree to Disagree

1. Write a list of grievances
2. Meet in a neutral location
3. Give everyone the opportunity to speak
4. Work it out
5. End on a positive note of understanding
   Plan B: Negotiation Fails
   1. Move out

EVERY DAY AN EASY A

How to Do Your Own Laundry

Tools of the Trade

Laundry Basket
Before You Wash: Stain Remover
For Washing Machine:
Laundry Detergent
Liquid Fabric Softener
Liquid Bleach
For Dryer: Anti-Static Sheet

Time Log: 4 Hours

Clothing Preparation	30 Minutes
Wash	30 Minutes (read textbook)
Dryer	1 Hour (read textbook)
Folding	30 Minutes
Travel	30 Minutes

Speedbumps: Delays, Detours, and Distractions 1 Hour
- Machines are full and you will have to wait your turn
- Dryer doesn't work well, takes longer than expected

Steps to Success

Step 1. Separate Clothing into Four Piles

Pile 1. Whites

Pile 2. Bright colors and darks

Pile 3. Clothes that produce lint: Towels, sweatshirts, chenille, and flannel

Pile 4. Clothes that attract lint: Corduroy, velvets, and permanent-press clothes

Step 2. Close All Zippers and Empty All Pockets

Step 3. Pre-Treat Heavy Stains with a Stain Remover

Step 4. Remove Lint from Dryer's Lint Tray

The Washing Machine   Time: 30 Minutes

Step 5. Add Clothes and Close Lid

Step 6. Add Cleaning Products
Add detergent, fabric softener, and bleach to the dispenser. Measure out the right amount according to manufacturer's instructions.

Step 7. Choose Water Temperature for Wash Cycle
Cold water protect colors and darks from bleeding or fading, and avoids shrinkage

Warm or hot water for whites and durable fabrics like cotton (make sure they're preshrunk)

The Dryer   Time: 1 Hour

Step 8. Put Clothes and Anti-Static Sheet in Dryer
• Select correct drying temperature
• Low for delicates
• Medium for most fabrics and high for cotton

Step 9. Fold Clothes   Time: 30 Minutes

EVERY DAY AN EASY A

SUDOKO COLLEGE PUZZLES

Many college newspaper contains a daily Sudoko puzzle.
College students find them entertaining and challenging.

What is a Sudoko puzzle?
It's a grid 9 squares wide and 9 squares deep.

4					2	8	3	
	8		1		4			2
7		6		8		5		
1					7		5	
2	7		5				1	9
	3		9	4				6
		8		9		7		5
3			8		6		9	
	4	2	7					3

The lines of squares running horizontally are called rows, and
the lines running vertically are called columns.

The grid is further divided by the darker lines into
nine 3 X 3 square 'boxes

The Rules
Some of the squares already have numbers in them. Your task
is to fill in the blank squares. There's only one rule:
Each row, column and box must end up containing all of the
numbers from 1 to 9. Each number can only appear once in a
row, column or box.

SUDOKO PUZZLE STRATEGY
© By Paul Stephens

Here is Paul's strategy to solve a Sudoko puzzle:

1. Try slicing and dicing to solve any easy squares. Don't spend too long on it though.

2. Crosshatch the entire puzzle box-by-box, pencilling-in complete candidate lists.

3. Scan the puzzle for the following rules:

Single-square candidates within an area (row/column/box) - solve immediately.

Claims by a box - remove the claimed candidate from the same row/column in other boxes.

Pairs within an area - remove the pair squares candidates from other lists within that area.

Triples within an area - remove the triple candidates from others lists within that area.

4. Whenever you solve a square, immediately check and update all candidate lists in the same row, column and box.

5. Whenever you've updated a candidate list, check to see if one of the rules now applies (e.g. you've created a triple, or a box is now claiming a number).

6. Never guess. Use logic. Have fun.

What If you could solve just one problem
in this world and by solving that one problem
you could solve every problem in the world?

If we just solve the "problem of education,"
then we could solve every problem in the
world: poverty, illiteracy, domestic violence,
religious strife, and war.

The human brain is the most powerful
biological machine in the world. What
would the world look like if educators
knew how to nurture and cultivate the
awesome power of the human brain?

When the seeds of peace are planted
within the minds and hearts of our children,
through education, then and only then,
will there be peace on earth. Our children
are our only hope for peace in the world,
and education is the only path to peace.

Sharon Rose Sugar

The Paladin of Education for the 21st Century

THIS BOOK SAVES LIVES

"The Silent Crisis Destroying America's Brightest Minds"
"Book of the Month" Alma Public Library, Wisconsin

About Us

SMARTGRADES
BRAIN POWER REVOLUTION

Sharon Rose Sugar

The Paladin of Education for the 21st Century

Critical Contributions to Education

1. **SMARTGRADES BRAIN POWER REVOLUTION**
2. Education Paradigm: The Learning-Processing Education System
3. 40 Universal Gold Standards of Education
4. How to Nurture and Cultivate the Power of the Human Brain
5. How Does Learning Take Place
6. How to Measure Education

7. 8 Goalposts of Education:
    1. EDUCATION: KNOWLEDGE!
    2. ENLIGHTENMENT: AHA!
    3. EMPOWERMENT: YES I CAN!
    4. EXCELLENCE: MASTERY!
    5. EMANCIPATION: ALL CAN DO!
    6. EGALITARIANISM: EQUAL RIGHTS!
    7. EQUALITY: NEW WORLD ORDER!
    8. ECONOMIC STABILITY: WORLD PEACE!

8. Integration Therapy for Intrapersonal Growth, Development and Maturity: 13 Steps to True and Everlasting Happiness

9. Feed the Whole Child: Mind, Body, and Spirit
10. Spiritual Affirmations: Empowerment, Responsibility, Special Gifts

11. The Silent Crisis Destroying America's Brightest Minds
    - 15 Stumbling Blocks of Academic Failure
    - 15 Stepping Stones to Academic Success
    - Downward Spiral of Academic Failure
    - Academic Insanity
    - Misdiagnosis of A.D.H.D., "The Incurable Brain Disorder"

12. 3 Stages of Child Abuse: Cripple, Parasite, and Predator

13. Coined Word, "Democrisy," a Democracy Laden with Hypocrisy

14. **PHOTON SUPERHERO OF EDUCATION**, PhotonSuperhero.com

15. C.A.P.S. Children's Science Curriculum, Grades 1-4
    (Content, Activity, Process, and Society)

16. In One Hour, Read Hebrew, HebrewPowerHour.com

Thinkers in Education

One Small Step for Women and
One Giant Leap Forward for
Education and World Peace.

Alain, Aristotle, Avicenna, Bello, Bettelheim, Binet,
Blonsky, Al-Boustani, Buber, Cai Yuanpei, Claparede,
Comenious, Condorcet, Confucius, Cousinet, Dawid,
Decroly, Dewey, Diesterweg, Durkheim, Eotvos,
Erasmus, Al-Farabi, Ferriere, Freinet, Freire, Freud,
Frobel, Fukuzawa, Gandhi, Al-Ghazali, Giner de
los Rios, Glinos, Goodman, Gramsci, Grundtvig,
Grzegorzewska, Hegel, Herbart, Humbolt, Husen,
Hussein, Illich, Jaspers, Jovellanos, Jullien de Paris,
Kandel, Kant, Kerschensteiner, Key, Ibn Khaldun,
Kold, Korczak, Krupskaya, Locke, Makarenko, Marti,
Mencious, Miskawayh, Montaigne, Montessori,
More, Naik, Neill, Noikov, Nyerere, Ortega y
Gasset, Owen, Pestalozzi, Piaget, Plato, Priestley,
Al-Qabbani, Read, Rogers, Rousseau, Rudenschold,
Sadler, Salomon, Sarmiento, Sergio, Skinner,
Spencer, Steiner, Suchodolski,

**Sharon Rose Sugar (Sharon Esther Lampert)
PHOTON SUPERHERO OF EDUCATION,**
Sun Yat-Sen, Tagore, Al-Tahtawi, Tolstoy, Trefort,
Trstenjak, Ushinsky, Uznadze, Varela, Vasconcelos,
Vico, Vives, Vygotsky, Wallon

My Superhero Pledge for World Peace

"I Pledge to Safeguard Your Mental Health,
Promote Mental Health in Your Family,
Create an Atmosphere of Peace Among Your Friends,
Inspire Good Will Among Your Neighbors, and
Build a Foundation of Stability in Your Community."

PHOTON
SUPERHERO OF EDUCATION
WWW.BOOKSNOTBOMBS.COM

EVERYBODY IS SOMEBODY SPECIAL

The Official Emblem of

PHOTON

Super Hero Refresher Course

Clark Kent Is Superman

Bruce Wayne Is Batman

Peter Parker Is Spiderman

Diana Themyscira Is Wonder Woman

Sharon Rose Sugar Is Photon

Does Your Kid Read Sharon Esther Lampert?

Critical Contributions to Civilization

The Prodigy
Unleash The Creator The God Within
10 Esoteric Laws of Genius & Creativity

The Awesome Art of Alliteration
Using One Letter of the Alphabet

The Prophet
Who Knew God Was Such a Chatterbox

THE 22 COMMANDMENTS
All You Will Ever Need to Know About God

The Philosopher Queen
- God of What? 11 Esoteric Laws of Inextricability
- The Sperm Manifesto: 10 Rules for the Road
- Women Have All The Power —
  But Have Never Learned How to Use It

The Poet
- I Stole All The Words from The Dictionary

- **IMMORTALITY IS MINE**
  The Greatest Poems Ever Written on Extraordinary World Events

- **POETRY JEWELS**
  Diamonds, Emeralds, Sapphires, Rubies, and Pearls

- **V.E.S.S.E.L.**
  Very. Extra. Special. Sharon. Esther. Lampert.

How to Read a Poem By Sharon Esther Lampert

1. Similar to the poet William Blake, Sharon's poems are accompanied by elaborate visual graphics that enrich and compliment the text.

2. Sharon is a master of the art of condensation. She is able to condense a major world event in world history into a one page poem.

3. Sharon's poems are telescopic of the main event and microscopic of the infinite details.

4. Sharon's poems are known for her ability to weave poetry, philosophy, and comedy into a single verse.

5. Sharon's poems take you on a cinematic journey, and make you feel as if you are reliving the event, as if it happened today.

6. Many poets leave abandoned poems, that are unfinished. Sharon's poems are completed works of art. Every word is essential to the poem. You cannot remove or replace a word. There are no extra words. Every word has its rightful place and fits to perfection.

7. Sharon's poems are inspired. There are no rough drafts. Like giving birth to a baby, the poem incubates in her "creative apparatus" and is birthed in minutes. Like a baby, the poems are delivered whole and complete.

8. The last verse of every poem delivers a message that educates, enlightens, and empowers. Her searing signature endings seep under your skin, and find a way into your heart, and open your mind to a deeper understanding of the world.

Letter from Mommy, Age 9
Darling Sharon,
My Daughter is a Poet, Philosopher,
and Teacher.
Beauty & Brains.
Love and Kisses, XXX
Mommy (Eve Lampert)

SHARON ESTHER LAMPERT

The Sole Intention of My Poetry
Is to Add Light to Your Soul.

Sharon Esther Lampert

PHOTON
SUPERHERO of EDUCATION®
EVERY DAY AN EASY A
SMARTGRADES
EVERY DAY AN EASY A
WE ARE THE FUTURE
EVERYBODY IS SOMEBODY SPECIAL

PHOTON
EVERY DAY AN EASY A

Dark Ages Despair.
PHOTON Is Here.

Enlightenment Is Her Destiny.
World Peace Is Her Legacy.

Nurture the Human Brain.
Keep Planet Earth Sane.

Ignorance Is the Enemy.
Education Is the Remedy.

SMARTGRADES
SCHOOL NOTEBOOKS
Will Prevail.
No Student Will Fail.

Students and Educators Are a Team.
Good Grades Become Grand Dreams.

Ignorance Is Bitter Not Bliss.
I Seal this Promise with a Kiss.

BUY NOW!
AMAZON 2 DAY SHIP
GLOBAL BOOKSTORES

EVERY DAY AN EASY A
TOTAL RECALL
YOUR STUDY ROOM IS UNDER NEW MANAGEMENT
SMARTGRADES SCHOOL NOTEBOOKS AND ACADEMIC PLANNER

EVERYBODY IS SOMEBODY SPECIAL
www.BooksNotBombs.com

www.ingramcontent.com/pod-product-compliance
Lightning Source LLC
Chambersburg PA
CBHW060906140726

47996CB00001B/144